POLICE WORK

Peter B. Ainsworth

Lecturer, Department of Social Administration,
University of Manchester

and

Ken Pease

Senior Lecturer, Department of Social Administration,
University of Manchester

Page 9,11,13,18,19 21 22
20

Published by The British Psychological Society
and Methuen
London and New York

First published in 1987 by The British Psychological Society, St Andrews House, 48 Princess Road East, Leicester LE1 7DR, in association with Methuen & Co. Ltd, 11 New Fetter Lane, London EC4P 4EE, and in the USA by Methuen, Inc., 29 West 35th Street, New York NY 10001.

British Library Cataloguing in Publication Data

Ainsworth, Peter B.
Police work. — (Psychology in action)
1. Police psychology
I. Title II. Pease, Ken III. British Psychological Society IV. Series
150'.243632 HV7936.P75

ISBN 0-901715-45-X
ISBN 0-901715-44-1 Pbk

Set in Compugraphic Mallard
by AB Printers Limited, 33 Cannock Street, Leicester LE4 7HR
Printed and bound in Great Britain by A. Wheaton & Co. Ltd., Exeter

PSYCHOLO IN ACTION

Psychology r s great deal to say about how we can make our working lives effective and rewarding: the way we see er people, how they see us, and our ability to communicate others and achieve what we want from a situation. Starting actual practice in the classroom, the police station, the y or the interviewing room, PSYCHOLOGY IN ACTION t the everyday working methods and concerns of ar groups of people and asks: where and how can gy help?

OUND TO THE SERIES

ries is an amalgam of two proposals made independently tish Psychological Society, one by Antony J. Chapman ny Gale, the other by John Radford and Ernest Govier. Psychological Society's Books and Special Projects ught the teams together to work out the main of the PSYCHOLOGY IN ACTION series, in n with the Society's Business and Publications The four originators have taken editorial responsibility t volumes in the series. This third title is edited by A.J. Chapman and A. Gale.

To Stanley Ainsworth and Nicholas Pease

Acknowledgements

We wish to thank Jackie Boardman and Enid Roberts for deciphering our scribble, Sandra Coward for her help with some of the examples in Chapter 2, Graeme Gerrard, who kindly read and commented on many of the draft chapters, Brian Gresty for long hours talking about the effects of experience in police work, and Helen Reeves for invaluable comments on a draft of Chapter 13.

PBA would like to thank Dr M.R. Chatterton for his guidance and inspiration over many years.

CONTENTS

Chapter 1

The Police and Psychology

The scene is the interview room of a police station. A sullen youth
of 16 faces a grey-haired sergeant. 'I'll never tell you nothing, cop-
per', he snarls. The sergeant replies 'I knew your mum, son. She was
a good 'un. What would she think if she could see you now?' The
boy pauses, breaks down in tears, and the background harmonica
music wells up. Sergeant Dixon is on his way to another triumph.

The most popular fictional British policeman of all time was television's PC Dixon of Dock Green. Before the end of each episode,
George Dixon would give homely advice to his audience on child
care, courteous driving and almost everything except gardening and
dress sense. The image was that of a kindly and street-wise friend
of the people, one whose long experience had taught him what to
do and how to do it in his service to the public. In truth, towards
the end of the programme's run, the wrinkles Dixon used in his job
were matched by the wrinkles on his face. He looked like the oldest
serving police officer in Britain.

A real-life George Dixon, even if he were to survive for long in the
service, would probably not feel he had much to learn from text-
books on psychology. He would probably argue that he had survived
on his wits for a lifetime and that common sense was good enough
for him. He would argue that police officers spend much of their
time in contact with members of the public and have worked out for
themselves what makes people tick. We would have to agree with
Dixon that the people who have the most relevant experience are
police officers and this experience should not be undervalued.
Nonetheless, officers currently in the police service are ready also to
acknowledge the findings of psychological research as both relevant
and useful.

One of us, a former police officer now trained as a psychologist,

(Ainsworth)

recently undertook a survey of nearly 200 police officers from four different forces in England and found that almost 90 per cent of them believed that psychology was of some value to the serving police officer. They identified particular tasks, like training and the handling of hostage or siege situations, where psychology is of particular relevance. But this recognition of psychology's value was not complete. We would argue that there are areas of particular relevance other than those identified by the officers questioned. Interestingly, the survey also showed a sex difference in police attitudes to psychology. Female officers had a more negative view of psychology than their male counterparts. We have ideas on why this might be so, and these you can read about in Chapter 8.

Given that there is no substitute for 'on the ground' experience as a police officer in handling difficult situations, what is the place that we claim for psychological research in helping the police officer to do his or her job? There is an old saying that having 30 years' experience is different from having one year's experience 30 times. Someone who finds a way of dealing with situations and sticks to it without exploring alternatives is not accumulating useful experience. In contrast, the psychologist attempts to study behaviour in a systematic way, often through the use of carefully controlled experiments, inside or outside the laboratory. By specifying alternatives and testing between them, courses of action can be identified as preferable in a way that is not otherwise possible. In this way psychologists have been able to offer understanding, help and advice to people in many situations. For example, educational psychologists bring to bear research on reading difficulties to help children in school. Clinical psychologists use strategies based on research to help those who have problems like stress, anxiety or depression.

Over recent years psychologists have also studied the workings of the criminal justice system generally and police work in particular. In addition to the particular relevance of the findings of such research, many other general psychological studies are both relevant and useful to policing, as we hope to demonstrate in the following chapters. Some, like evidence on the unreliability of eye-witness testimony, will have immediate practical application. Others, like evidence about when people help each other, are useful for police officers to know about, but we have to work harder to prove it.

Uncommon common sense

It is sometimes suggested that successful conduct of your life in interaction with other people is just a matter of common sense. Common sense may not be as common as we would like to think. What is common sense to one person may not be common sense to another. What we regard as common sense here may not be seen as common sense there. For instance, proverbs may be taken to constitute examples of common sense, but many proverbs contradict each other. Birds of a feather flock together but opposites attract; many hands make light work but too many cooks spoil the broth. Even when people assert that a particular outcome of a problem is common sense, psychological research often leads us to doubt whether this is really the case. Psychologists have researched the 'knew-it-all-along' effect. For example, if you were told the result of a soccer match, you would be confident that you could have predicted it. You would be more confident than you would have been if you had been asked to predict the result beforehand. Perhaps that is why people keep doing football pools. Looking back you can remember almost putting in the right matches on the treble chance. If only you had heeded your better judgement, you would be rich. You will not, of course, make the same mistake next Saturday. Another way of persuading yourself of the reality of the knew-it-all-along effect is to fall into conversation with people in a betting shop around 4.30 p.m. Historians are as bad as everyone else in this respect. In 1985, it is obvious common sense that William the Conqueror would beat King Harold at the Battle of Hastings. It was not so obvious to the seasick Frenchmen on their way to Hastings.

Knowing about the knew-it-all-along effect has helped us when teaching police officers. If you describe a piece of psychological research and ask officers how they think the results turned out, many get it wrong. This makes them less inclined to dismiss the real results as common sense.

The effect of environments

Psychologists often try to understand under what conditions people behave as they do, and thus go beyond the simple explanations which most people are usually ready to accept. Let us take an example. A man in a psychiatric hospital smashes a window on the ward where he is detained. When asked why he broke the window we could simply say 'because he is crazy'. To the psychologist and to many intelligent people in other walks of life, that is no explanation at all. We might ask, for example, why he did not break the window yesterday, or even an hour earlier, or in his own home, or on the other side of the ward? We might more generally ask whether this sort of behaviour in a hospital is typical of his behaviour outside it, and so gain some clues about the requirements of his detention in the first place. When we try to understand why people behave as they do, we must be aware of all the relevant factors, both internal and external.

The tendency to underestimate the effect of external conditions on people's behaviour is well established. The *over* estimation of the importance of the personality in behaviour and the *under* estimation of the importance of the environment appears very often in psychological research. Let us take rape as an example. People will tend to be biased in thinking that women who are raped have personality characteristics which contributed to what happened. Police officers may become irritated with witnesses who cannot give a clear account of an event, thereby underestimating the possible impact of the situation on the witness.

As the eminent American psychologist Elliot Aronson argues in his book *The Social Animal*, 'people who do crazy things are not necessarily crazy'. The effect of attaching labels to people in preference to thinking about the situations they are in serves to exclude people dismissed in such unflattering ways from proper contact with us normal people. Another possibility is that of denying the situational factors which have such a powerful impact on all our behaviour. It is too easy to say of a colleague we see interviewed on television 'I could do better than that', forgetting the intimidating and unreal atmosphere of the studio setting. A final danger is that by explaining behaviour in terms of personalities rather than situations we close off from ourselves opportunities for changing situations. This is a particular problem for crime prevention initiatives. People should not steal cars with poor locks, but while you concentrate on blaming and catching the offenders, you could also be encouraging the motor manufacturers to redesign their locks.

If you were asked the question 'Would you be prepared to administer an apparently fatal electric shock to a fellow human being who had merely answered a question wrongly?', most of you would say 'no'. The norms of our society tell us that this would be inappropriate if not inexcusable. In an experiment described fully in Chapter 6, it was found that nearly two-thirds of a sample of ordinary people were prepared to deliver electric shocks in this way merely because someone had told them to. It would be easy and comforting to be able to dismiss these people as 'crazy', yet they were normally-functioning human beings who had merely responded to the pressures of a particular situation.

An even more dramatic example is provided by events in Jonestown, Guyana, where almost a thousand people committed mass suicide on the orders of their leader. We may feel smug in the belief that these people must have been 'weird' or 'freaks' and that *we* would never do anything as bizarre as that. However, is the readiness of police officers to smoke cigarettes or juveniles to sniff glue much more than suicide in Russian roulette form? Perhaps the events in Jonestown can simply be regarded as Russian roulette with five full chambers. Occupational pressures on police officers are no less powerful, leading to occasions where officers behave in ways which are at least questionable. All experienced officers will remember times when they felt pressure to go against their moral principles in protecting a colleague's job or reputation, and will know how strong those pressures can be. They are mentioned again in the discussion on stress in Chapter 12.

Here is one final example of a situation in which common sense is likely to be in error. In this case, to avoid the knew-it-all-along effect we described earlier, try to guess the result of the following research. A man is walking down the street and suddenly falls to the ground clutching his chest and groaning. Is the man more likely to receive immediate help if one person witnessed the incident or if more than one person did so? Please guess now. Evidence from a series of studies (reviewed more fully in Chapter 5) suggests that, perhaps counter to what would pass for common sense, one potential 'Good Samaritan' is better than a number of them. There may be less safety in numbers than we care to suppose. However, there is no point in berating people for not coming to the help of another when that failure is the normal response. We should, to follow the logic described earlier, think about the problem in terms of the characteristics of the situation, not of the people involved.

Practical policing

Nobody, least of all the psychologist, conducts the whole of his or her life by the precepts of research psychology. However, we hope we have already provided some evidence to suggest that you should not live it by the feeling in your guts alone. There are predictable ways in which you will be wrong if you do so. A particular problem with police work arises as a result of its importance. Mistakes can have such disastrous consequences. The wrong assumption that a particular minicab driver was involved in drug dealing contributed as a flashpoint in the Brixton riots of 1981. A wrong choice of words to a would-be suicide can have fatal consequences. On a more mundane level, an offhand manner when giving directions to a member of the public can produce a sense of grievance in someone on whom a police officer may have to rely for information in the future (see Chapter 13). Research has demonstrated that the personal style of some police officers, as well as some citizens, leads them to get involved in violent encounters far more often than others. George Dixon would of course recognize how the situation limited the range of options available to an officer, and which of the available options to choose. The options available when dealing with drunk or angry people, for instance, will not be the same as when dealing with the sober and calm. The officer will also recognize how threatened loss of face will limit his or her options when dealing with a group of young people. Sensitivity of this sort is surely a requirement for efficient policing. The Metropolitan Police have recently adopted training packages which include psychology as part of their human awareness training (now 'Policing Skills') for recruits.

Psychologists point to the dangers of what is known as the 'self-fulfilling prophecy'. For example, if you believe that all flashers wear long dirty overcoats then it is likely that only people who wear this kind of clothing will come under suspicion. People dressed differently will be less likely to be arrested and so the statistics at the end of the year will be seen as proof of the accuracy of your belief in the universal uniform of the flasher. The example is not unique. Shoplifters and fraudsters are also in the category of offenders where self-fulfilling prophecies can operate. Shoplifters are well-dressed middle-aged women or poorly-dressed youngsters, the stereotype says. Confidence tricksters wear medallions, thick gold rings and drive Ford Sierras. Nor is the police officer or store detective alone in being in a position to fulfil their own predictions. For example, pathologists and coroners may classify corpses as suicides in doubtful cases on the basis of those social characteristics which are thought to be associated with suicide, like chronic illness or recent bereavement. If we are willing to have even our common sense beliefs and intuitions challenged, then we are much more likely to make the most of each new piece of experience, that precious commodity that money cannot buy.

It is a particularly human motive to want to understand ourselves and others. We want to know who and what we are, how we got that way, how we can change ourselves, what we have in common with other people and in what ways we are unique. This understanding of human beings and their behaviour is the foremost goal of psychology and one which we believe has considerable relevance for police officers in their profession as well as in their identity as human beings.

Some of the problems

Despite the brave words on professional relevance, there are gaps in our knowledge and in almost every area understanding is under revision. Psychological research on criminal justice is beset by many problems, both ethical and practical. Progress in psychology is fastest where the possibilities for research are greatest. Understanding of *memory* and *perception* is reasonably good because there are fewer ethical constraints on the kind of study which it is acceptable to carry out on these topics. In contrast the criminal justice system is obviously full of ethical limitations (both real and imagined) on what we may do. To take one example, the effectiveness of penal sanctions cannot be completely assessed because we cannot randomly allocate people to different experimental 'treatments' as one would in a laboratory experiment in psychology. Similarly, asking police officers to adopt a particular style of policing would be useful but unethical when suggested by psychologists (although reasonable when required by Chief Constables).

Whatever the views of some cynics, police officers are human beings, drawn from the ranks of the general public. So, research on people who have no police experience can still be of considerable relevance to those who happen to hold the office of constable. It is also true that police work is distinctive and that police officers develop characteristic ways of responding to situations. Our aim in this book is to balance the common and the distinctive. The reader will find descriptions of research both on police personnel and on other people. In reading it, police officers are required to believe that they are not a race apart, exempt from the general principles which govern human behaviour. They will find it less difficult to meet the other requirement, which is the recognition of the distinctiveness of police work and behaviour. In any event, the police work with the public. Even if there is a certain reluctance to accept that research on other people is relevant to police officers, there is no reluctance in assuming that the rules of behaviour apply to everyone else, and are in this indirect sense relevant to police work. We hope, of course, that police officers will not set themselves apart like this. They would be very foolish to do so.

This book explores only some of the topics of professional

relevance to the police officer. But we want to persuade you of the importance of understanding at least some psychology in your work, and we supply the basis for some of that understanding. We hope that the book will also develop an appetite in at least some readers for the application of more psychological research than we have mentioned. An idea of how many areas of psychological research are relevant to police work can be obtained from *Psychology for Police Officers*, by Ray Bull and his colleagues (1984). For those who do acquire the motivation to go further, we recommend that book.

Review notes

Common sense is not enough as a basis for good police work. People tend to overestimate what they could have predicted, and underestimate the pressures which environments exert on people. In these ways, and others, common sense is uncommon. Despite the many problems with psychological research, it already has much of value to offer the police officer. This book is intended as a simple introduction to some areas of psychology relevant to police work.

References

Aronson, E. (1984) *The Social Animal*. New York: Freeman.

Bull, R., Bustin B., Evans P., and Gahagan, D. (1984) *Psychology for Police Officers*. Chichester: Wiley.

Chapter 2

Getting through to people:
Non-verbal communication

One of the things that distinguishes humans from other animals is our ability to communicate through the use of language. Most of the knowledge we acquire in our lifetime is communicated through the language, spoken and written, of our particular culture. However, in a great number of our interactions with other people we pay as much attention to *how* people express themselves as we do to *what* they actually say. Psychologists have for many years studied the way in which we communicate and interact, and have focused particularly on the role of *Non-Verbal Communication* or NVC.

Each one of us, whether we are speaking or not, is 'communicating' with others – for instance, through the clothes we wear, the way we sit, the expression on our face. An observer will attend to these and many other aspects of NVC in order to come to understand the other person. Although speech is the predominant source of communication, the spoken word can rarely be fully understood without reference to other, non-verbal aspects. A person may say something which sounds hurtful, though we realize the comment is meant as a joke when we see the broad accompanying smile. We seem to be able to 'sense' when someone is telling us lies – what we are probably picking up are subtle changes of posture and gesture which alert us to the fact that another person is feeling uncomfortable.

Quite often we learn the rules of communicating and use non-verbal signals without thinking about them. It is only when we meet someone who does not conform to the rules that we realize how crucial some aspects are. For example, we 'automatically' look at another person when we are conversing with them. But suppose while talking to another person you were aware that she was staring at your right ear, rather than glancing at your eyes. All the other person has done is shifted their gaze two or three degrees to the left, but the effect is quite startling and dramatic. (It's a simple experiment you can try!) A person who stares at our ear will be seen as strange, or weird, or we will quickly become very uncomfortable and wonder why we are being treated in this unusual way, perhaps touching our ear to find out whether there is food or dirt on it. The point is that even slight breaches of the rules of NVC can very quickly disrupt smooth communicative flow. This point has been taken up by a number of psychologists, who now offer training in social skills to a whole range of people, including the mentally ill.

We feel that as a great deal of police officers' time is spent interacting with members of the public it makes sense for these officers to develop their social skills. The Metropolitan Police already give some basic training in this area, under the title 'Policing Skills', and many other forces cover the topic while teaching officers to conduct interviews. However, NVC operates at a relatively low level of awareness – we are often unaware of exactly what signals we are giving off or receiving. A whole host of things make up NVC and in this chapter we discuss some of the more important.

Context

If we are to make sense of any piece of behaviour we must understand the context in which it occurs. Consider the difference between a police officer's behaviour when stopping a motorist for speeding, and when appearing before a senior officer on a discipline charge. In the first instance the officer will be in obvious charge of the situation – his or her stance, gestures and overall general manner will communicate this to the motorist. Now consider the same police officer facing the discipline charge. Although he or she is the same individual the whole behaviour will be considerably different. The head may well be bowed (a submissive gesture) the body will be tense and stiff. The point is that our behaviour is determined to a considerable degree by the context in which it occurs. We communicate with others very differently in, say, a doctor's surgery, a church or a courtroom. A police officer may appear friendly and approachable when showing children across the road, but authoritative and aggressive when the pubs are emptying on a Saturday night. These attitudes are generally communicated non-verbally in the first instance. The police officer will obviously also pay attention to context when judging the attitudes or styles of others. He or she may feel that a particular individual does not fit in to a particular location and question the person to ascertain whether their business is legitimate.

KINESICS

Kinesics is an umbrella heading used to describe many aspects of NVC which are further divided as follows.

Static features

A person's face even when viewed statically can convey a vast array of information. It will reveal racial category, a rough estimate of age, sex, etc. Although the face is not an accurate guide to personality or intelligence, we often assume it to be so. For example, one psychologist showed people photographs of faces and asked them to describe the personalities of the people depicted. They were quite prepared to do this, and their descriptions were often uniform, suggesting that there are facial stereotypes. Psychologists have shown that people with very attractive faces are assumed to lead happier and more interesting lives than people with unattractive faces. There are also implications for court appearances. For example, mock juries have been found to be more likely to convict unattractive people than attractive people even when the evidence presented is the same. Not only the face, but also a person's physique may give clues to the person's personality – or so many people think. We may assume fat people to be jolly, thin people to be nervous, and so on. We may also have stereotyped views about criminals and their typical appearance. You may have completely different images of the 'typical' person likely to commit armed robbery, compared with the 'typical' person who may commit an indecent exposure. These images may have some validity though we must be wary of the self-fulfilling prophecy referred to in Chapter 1.

Psychologists have also studied the amount of information which may be conveyed by a person's voice. Usually we can identify a speaker's national or regional origin. We also like to think we can tell something about intelligence and personality from the voice, though as with the previous two examples, we may simply be responding to stereotyped views. Be that as it may, there is some evidence that the pitch of a person's voice tends to rise during deception.

Although we inevitably attend to small details when assessing another person, we tend to combine all the information to build up an overall impression. For example, psychologists showed many years ago that a person who wears glasses is perceived as more intelligent than a person who does not. However, when we are given a larger sample of the bespectacled person's behaviour, this effect of spectacles becomes less pronounced. One experiment in the USA has also shown that traffic police officers are perceived more negatively when wearing mirror sunglasses, and that people being reported for an offence are likely to be more aggressive towards officers wearing a gun.

The clothes we wear can even be said to constitute an aspect of NVC, as can hairstyles, make up, etc. We cannot do very much about static features of our faces, short of plastic surgery. What we choose to wear and decorate ourselves with is likely to represent a communicative effort. Whilst it is obvious that these are highly significant cues there has been little systematic research on them. Police officers, like other people, may use clothes and hairstyles as a guide to categorizing people or even stereotyping them. Many groups deliberately adopt certain styles to signify their allegiance to a particular group (for example, skinheads, punks, vicars). Clothes, make up and hairstyles are important because they are used as a means of telling others how we see ourselves and how we want others to see us. We would remind the reader, however, that stereotyping a person because of appearance has its problems. Not all people with long hair and scruffy clothes are drug takers (see Chapter 8)!

On the subject of clothes we must also mention that a police uniform generally tends to convey a great deal to a member of the public. Some members of the public will feel reassured by the presence on the street of a uniformed officer, while others may feel uncomfortable or hostile. It is a rare individual who reacts completely neutrally to the sight of a police uniform. The appearance immediately signifies authority – which some people will respect and others challenge. Status is conveyed by the wearing of a uniform, especially by an officer of senior rank. Psychologists have shown that people of high status are more effective 'persuaders', hence there may be some merit in having a high ranking officer interview a difficult suspect. The potential power of a high status authority figure is illustrated in the experment by Stanley Milgram described in Chapter 6.

We hope to show in this section that even when people think they are doing nothing they are 'giving off' non-verbal signals which alert others to what they may expect. The problem with these signals is that many of them (for example, physique) are out of our control. In the next section we look at some factors which may be more easily controlled by the individual.

Dynamic cues

Psychologists have carried out a great deal of research into the non-verbal cues used during an interaction between two people. We usually have a conversation with another person without even thinking about our posture, gesture, or eye contact yet these are crucial to any interaction. We consider here some of the more important aspects.

Orientation. When two people are interacting they can stand or sit at various angles to each other – head on, side by side, at right angles, etc. It appears that we tend to choose different angles depending on the type of encounter we are expecting. For example, if we are anticipating a competitive encounter, we would choose to sit opposite another person, whereas if we are planning to cooperate we would tend to sit side by side. Similarly, if we are expecting a friendly encounter we would choose a position allowing more proximity than when we expect an unfriendly encounter (where we would choose a position further away). A police officer conducting an interrogation of a suspect must pay close attention to the orientation taken relative to the suspect's in order for the interaction to be effective. It is less easy for a suspect to be evasive when faced directly by the interrogating officer. How we sit or stand is obviously important but so too is *where* we choose to put ourselves. Psychological studies have shown that status and leadership in a group is related to choice of position. We can usually make an informed guess about who is influential in a group by examining the positions which group members have chosen. For example, we would expect high status people to sit at the head of the table where they were in a position of visual control over others.

Distance and personal space. We may often be unaware of the distance rules in interactions – until someone breaks them. Have you ever had a conversation with someone who insisted on standing too close or too far away? There are cultural norms about what are appropriate distances for interactions but there are also some individual differences. Edwin Hall has suggested that there are four distances at which people interact, which correspond to four types of character. Intimate friends interact at distances of 0–30 inches, casual friends at 30–48 inches. People in 'social-consultative' encounters interact at 4–12 feet, whilst distances greater than 12 feet would indicate a public encounter. We all have notions of 'personal space', defined by Robert Sommer as 'an area with invisible boundaries surrounding a person's body into which intruders may not come'.

Psychologists have consistently demonstrated that invasion of our personal space typically makes us feel uncomfortable. For example, an American psychologist conducted an experiment in a university library where she deliberately sat next to a reader and moved her chair very close (despite the fact that there were many other seats available). The people whose personal space was invaded in this way showed their discomfort by getting up from their place quite quickly. A more dramatic example was provided by a more controversial experiment. A men's toilet was chosen as the unlikely location for this research. The experimenter waited until a man entered the toilet, which contained a row of urinals. The experimenter (also male, in case you wondered) then stood deliberately close to him. The effect of this invasion of personal space was that men tended to spend less time urinating than when they were not subjected to this intrusion.

Personal space is a vital aspect of all interactions. A police officer simply talking to a member of the public on the street will convey a different message depending upon the distance at which he or she stands. A police officer who 'feels someone's collar' is directly invading their personal space, and eyeball-to-eyeball confrontations do not need words to convey a message. A search represents a different kind of intrusion of the personal space boundary.

The notion of normal interpersonal distance is also important in conducting interviews or interrogations. A police officer who knowingly invades another's personal space will make that person uncomfortable before anything is said. Indeed one book suggests that the officer should 'move his chair in closer so that ultimately one of the subject's knees is just about in between the interrogator's two knees'. Whether this should apply whatever the gender of the officer and suspect is not supplied, nor is it said what one should do with the ensuing accusation of indecent assault if it does! Attempts to move a chair away, or lean back, indicate a totally understandable unwillingness to cooperate, and the tactic advocated seems to us to constitute undue pressure.

If loss of personal space is unavoidable (for example, in a crowded lift or bus) the polite thing to do is to try to compensate by other non-verbal means, like standing rigidly, avoiding eye contact by (in the case of the lift) staring intently at the floor indicator, and talking to people you know in a slightly louder voice than is strictly necessary, to show that really you are behaving in ways appropriate to the proper personal distancing. Deliberately not doing this is a clear

challenge or invitation. At the start of a boxing match, as the comba-
tants are being instructed by the referee, perhaps they do need to
stand close together. But do they really need to face each other
squarely and engage in unblinking eye contact? Clearly they do not,
and a challenge is mutely offered in this display.

Furniture arrangement. We saw earlier how people choose different
seats depending upon the type of encounter they have in mind. Even
such details as the shape of a table or the positioning of chairs will
influence patterns of communication. A circular table will tend to
enhance free discussion, whereas a rectangular one will confer expectations that the person who sits at the head will be the leader.
One look at a typical courtroom will tell you something about status
and power. Judges generally sit in an elevated position ('above' the
other people in the court), and behind them (both literally and
metaphorically) is the royal coat of arms, showing that the power of
the state is backing them up. The prosecution and defence will be
on the same level, confirming their status as equals. The dock res-
tricts the prisoner, and, particularly in older courts, gives the impression of a person with whom you cannot take any chances. In
contrast, court officials move more freely around their furniture.
There are status overtones to the instruction to attendant officers, on
a defendant's conviction, to 'take the prisoner down'.

   Furniture arrangements can also tell us something about the person who normally occupies a certain room. For example, different
messages are conveyed by people who sit with their backs to the
door, compared with people who sit facing it. In the latter case, the
person can establish immediate eye contact with anyone entering
the room, whereas in the former someone entering would be unsure
how to start a conversation, or when.

   A person of high status (for example, a Chief Constable) may convey his or her authority symbolically by sitting behind a large, imposing desk. Anyone entering the office has to face 'the great one'
across this imposing desk, probably from the comfort of a lower
chair than that occupied by the great one. This is a mixed blessing
from the perspective of the great one. What he or she gains in obvious status, is lost in the capacity to intrude into the other's personal
space. Of course, some 'great ones' conspicuously come out from behind their desk-barrier to a part of their large office where they can
sit (not opposite, that would look too competitive) with their guest,
just as though they were equal. This sort of tactic with furniture, of
course, gives off messages of its own. John Walkley suggests that the

face-to-face across a table seating arrangement is a particularly bad one for an interrogation. It allows a suspect to conceal body movements, and also makes communication difficult and inescapably competitive.

It often appears that interviews can be made more or less stressful for participants depending on the furniture arrangements. For example, the typical promotion selection board might involve an officer entering a large room and having to head for the one hard uncomfortable seat placed in the middle of the floor. The interviewing officers are arranged in a semi-circle partly hidden by desks. This furniture arrangement, which is completely uncompromising in the status messages it gives, is almost guaranteed to intimidate the interviewee, who is, and feels, 'on the spot'; is under almost constant eye gaze; cannot conceal any of his or her actions behind a screening table – and has nothing to do with his or her hands. This type of seating arrangement adds tension to an already stressful experience. We are also reminded of the old charge office desk where the receiving sergeant would be seated very high up and be able to peer down at the prisoner being accepted. No doubt you can think of many other examples where the arrangement of the furniture carries a clear messsage which anyone in the situation will respond to. We discuss other ways in which the physical environment affects behaviour in Chapter 7.

Posture. The way in which we hold ourselves, whether standing or sitting, can convey a great deal. People may adopt an 'open' or a 'closed' posture by the positioning of their arms, legs and even head. Posture offers clues as to whether people are attentive or uninterested, whether they are nervous or relaxed. Posture is often a good clue to whether one person likes or fears another. There are, superimposed on these individual differences, cultural norms governing 'appropriate' postures. For instance, it may be considered normal to slouch in an open, relaxed posture at the cinema, but not in church. In a group, people may vary their postures so as to make them 'fit' or otherwise with those of others present. If one person deliberately adopts a different posture (perhaps leaning back with hands linked behind the head whilst others are attentively leaning forward), this may be the equivalent of detaching from the group. Posture is yet another reflection of status. Erving Goffman observing a staff meeting at a psychiatric hospital noted that the high status personnel would sit relaxed and in the front row, whereas the more junior staff adopted more formal postures in seats nearer the back of the room. This is particularly evident in the courtroom, where the languid poses of counsel contrast with the prim postures of those unfamiliar with the environment. Of course, if the defendant looks relaxed, that verges on 'dumb insolence'. An interesting phrase, that, only possible in the light of the kind of thing we are talking about in this chapter.

The way people stand or sit is thus partly governed by cultural norms, as well as reflecting status, personality and emotional state. A police officer may well claim to be able to recognize a prostitute or a 'troublemaker' simply from their posture. What the officer may not realize is that they themselves give off clues to their occupation (even when off duty or in plain clothes) by adopting a distinctive posture. One of us recalls an experience with a class from the Royal Ulster Constabulary attending a course he was teaching at the University of Ulster. It has a tragic end, and is recounted in a spirit of sad affection. At the start of the course an inspector instructed the officers not to dress distinctively and try to be inconspicuous among the students, because the lecture room could not be made fully secure. Yet seeing those officers among students at the coffee bar before lectures, they stood out as clearly as if they had been in uniform, by dint of bearing, manner of dress, and the bulge of their weapons. The class following theirs was bombed, and officers died. There were other ways besides their appearance by which they could have been known to attend classes by those who committed the outrage, so no direct cause–effect relationship could be inferred – but they certainly could not rely on their inconspicuousness.

Posture can often be a good way of checking on whether we can believe what a person is saying. Studies have shown that there are differences in body posture and movements when people are lying and when they are telling the truth. For example, an apparently relaxed person may suddenly cross their legs or arms when lying. The successful 'con-man' may well have learned to minimize the body cues which might give him away. Most of us have not, and that is why our true feelings 'leak' into our behaviour. Experiments have been carried out in which people were asked to judge whether patients were hiding their true feelings about problems they were having. Half of these people were able to view the patient's entire body and its movements, whereas the others could only see the face and head. The researchers found that the people who saw only the head and face were much more likely to be deceived as to the true feelings expressed than were the subjects who could attend to body cues as well. This is a good example of how people are able to control their facial expressions but may be less able to control their posture.

A more recent experiment has shown that the relationship between non-verbal signals and deceit is rather a complex one. The experiment showed, for example, that lies told by women were more easily detected than lies told by men; also, it was easier to detect lies when the subject and the observer were of opposite sex. This interesting experiment also suggested that non-verbal behaviour may be most likely to give away a lie when the subject's motivation is high and confidence low. We would suggest that both these conditions are likely to prevail when a person is being interrogated. Even if the start of interrogation is accompanied by arms-folded defiance and hostility, it may progress through a stiffening of the posture as tension increases, to a bowing of the head and spreading of the arms in a clear signal of submission or defeat. However, a submissive interviewee is not an unmixed blessing, as the large and troubling history of experiences with false confessions bears witness.

Gestures. Gestures can tell us much about another person and are used extensively to communicate. Head nods, handshakes (occasionally with a little highly communicative pressure of the thumb) and fist shaking are used both when speech is not possible or to accompany speech, when they are termed 'illustrators'. In the latter case the hands or head may be used to accentuate or emphasize a word or phrase. The speaker may use a whole variety of these illustrators, ranging from a slight inclination of the upper body to fist banging to accompany an emphatic point. As with many aspects of NVC, we may not be consciously aware of just how important gestures can be as means of communication. You may wish to try turning down the sound on your TV set (not during a play, that would be cheating), and looking at the gestures which speakers use. It is often easy to get an impression of what is being said even though the words cannot be heard. A person who is skilled at noticing gestures will be at an advantage when it comes to interviewing. Many gestures can give away when a person may be lying or starting to feel uncomfortable as an important area is probed. Wringing the hands and tugging at earlobes provide examples of possible indicators, as can other acts of self-manipulation. An involuntary nod of the head or a wry smile at an interviewer's remark should also not pass unnoticed. While there is a skill in simply seeing these signs, and while they are grist for the mill of interpretation, it is important to remember that they are not magic. Only an Inspector Clouseau would judge a lie simply by earlobe tugging.

A digression on polygraphs

Many of the examples given above and in the following pages suggest that a person may give an indication that he or she is starting to feel uncomfortable by changing posture or gesture. This is usually but not always an involuntary act caused by an increase in tension. There have been attempts to measure tension by direct physiological indicators. It is clearly sensible to try to do this, on the basis that direct indices may be less prone to disguise by conscious effort. These instruments (usually now known simply as polygraphs) monitor changes in breathing, heart rate and sweat activity in the skin. Millions of polygraph tests have been carried out in the USA. Emotional responsiveness to questions, the theory goes, reveals the true state of affairs, so that, for example, a 'yes' answer associated with high physiological measures may mean the real answer is 'no'. The use across the Atlantic, often for employee selection, has not been reflected in the UK. If the technique were foolproof, it would be an obvious boon to investigating officers. But it is not foolproof. The technique is basically unreliable. We are right not to use it (see Bull, 1983).

One technique of questioning may be an *incidental* benefit of the work on polygraphs. This is to ask a series of neutral questions and observe a particular person's characteristic way of responding to them. This establishes a base line against which to gauge the NVC linked with answers to questions which sound non-threatening, but whose significance only the offender is in a position to recognize. Even here, caution must be exercised, because if the questioner's NVC changes when it comes to the crucial questions, it may be that rather than the question content to which the suspect responds. That said, as John Waltman (1983) notes, a base line is vital because:

> One individual might act differently from others under identical circumstances. In addition, since interrogation is likely to be a very tense situation, an officer detecting nervous behaviour needs to be able to gauge whether that behaviour is a product of the situation or of the question currently being considered.

Facial expression. We discussed earlier how the face can convey information about the person behind it. The face is also an important means of communicating emotion. There is strong psychological evidence to support the notion of universality of expressing emotions in facial expression. We can recognize the expression of basic emotions like anger, happiness and fear no matter what the cultural background of the person concerned. We must be careful, though. Different cultures have different rules about when you should express emotion, so the absence of the relevant facial expression is by no means conclusive evidence of the absence of the emotion itself. Nor must the face be considered independently of everything else. Sarcasm is recognized by the inconsistency between what is said and the accompanying facial expression. Harsh words from a smiling mouth give a distinctive message.

Psychologists have pointed out how a speaker may raise the eyebrows at the same time as a word is stressed. The listener may also give off signals to convey that he or she understands, approves or is puzzled by what is being said. Again we would emphasize how the skilled interrogator must learn to attend closely to small variations in facial expression if he or she is to pick up the all-important clues given off by a person being interviewed. We should also be aware of how important our own facial expressions are to people with whom we have to communicate. A member of the public is virtually certain to be more helpful to a police officer who is perceived as friendly and approachable than to an officer who appears aggressive or threatening.

Gaze direction and eye contact. Extensive work has been carried out by psychologists demonstrating how important eye contact can be in facilitating communication. We noted earlier how difficult it can be to have a conversation with someone who insists on staring at our ear. What is remarkable is just how good we are at telling whether someone is looking at our eyes. Typically, listeners look at speakers' eyes for a large proportion of the time, much more than speakers look at listeners' eyes. However, eye gaze is broken up into small chunks of a few seconds, except when the tone of the exchange is intimate or challenging. In conversation, eye gaze serves two main functions, *observation* and *signalling*. It has been shown that a person looks less at someone who is disliked or is felt to be inferior, or if the topic of conversation is difficult or embarrassing. Most people also tend to look less, or not at all, if they are lying. It is very difficult to look someone unflinchingly in the eye and lie. An averting of eyes (typically downwards) is often a clue that we pick up when trying to establish if someone is telling the truth. Looking at someone directly whilst lying is very stressful for most people and even if eye contact is maintained, the stress may well show itself in some other gesture or body movement designed to release tension.

Eye contact is crucial in regulating the interchange during conversation. When someone is coming to the end of what they wanted to say, they look directly at the other person. This is a signal to the listener that the speaker has finished and the listener is being invited to take a turn as speaker. If the first speaker does not give this signal (by looking up) at the end of an utterance, the other person will take appreciably longer to start a reply. If the listener speaks before the speaker looks up, this may be construed as an interruption. Gaze is also used as a sign about liking/disliking. The longer the gaze, the better the liking, in general terms. Some psychologists have suggested that there is an appropriate level of intimacy for any encounter. This is maintained partly by the amount of mutual gaze. If one participant wishes to make the encounter more intimate they may gaze more. This may be reciprocated or rejected by the other person by increasing or decreasing their own amount of gaze.

The suggestion of an 'appropriate' level of eye contact is an important one. Between two strangers a long gaze would be perceived as a hostile and threatening signal, especially if the two strangers were face to face. The staring threat is shared by many animals, who will try to stare each other out until one signals submission by lowering the eyes. One police officer we know thinks that more men avert their gaze from him when he is in uniform! Boxers who stand staring only inches away from each other represent a clear attempt at intimidation, and if either contestant 'forces' the other to look down (and lose face) this is seen as some kind of victory. Police officers may be only too aware of the number of times a pub fight may have been started by one stranger objecting to another's stares: 'Who are you staring at?' A person who *wants* to dominate another will thus tend to stare for longer periods. This act may well serve to tell the other person 'I'm in charge of this interaction'. The police officer patrolling the streets can use this technique to his or her advantage when the need to control an incident arises.

We can see that eye contact and direction of gaze can signal a great deal to another person – yet we are rarely aware of consciously controlling this process. We may pick up the signal if someone 'gives us the eye' or be inquisitive about someone who 'gives us a funny look'. In fact when a police officer sees someone whom he or she 'does not like the look of', or someone who appears to be behaving suspiciously, it is very often non-verbal behaviour rather than talk which gives rise to that impression. The officer who claims to possess a sixth sense for sniffing out troublemakers is generally just sensitive to such signs as, for instance, a person averting their gaze quickly from the officer's. Customs officials may have a similar acute awareness of the subtle behaviours of the nervous passenger trying to smuggle in an extra bottle of Scotch.

A final clue given by the eyes is pupil size. The size of the pupil increases when a person is looking at things they are excited by. One psychologist investigated whether people use pupil size as a factor in reaching first impressions of people. Men were shown a photograph of an attractive woman and asked to give their reaction to her. In fact half the men saw a photograph where the woman's pupils had been touched up to make them appear slightly larger. The photographs were identical in all other respects. The experimenter found that men preferred women with larger pupils! It is interesting to note that people (men, at least) do react to differences in pupil size, yet even when questioned about it, they seem unaware of the thing that had the effect.

Territories

We described earlier how people exhibit a need for a certain amount of 'personal space' and feel uncomfortable when this space is invaded. It is also true that people, like some other animals, will actively seek to defend what they take to be their own territory. The expression 'an Englishman's home is his castle' may be sexist and hackneyed, but it is backed up by the law. Legislation permits a householder to defend his or her property against intrusion by others, including the police, to whom he or she is entitled to say 'You're not coming in without a warrant'. Territorial behaviour can take on great importance and be a source of great conflict, as many police officers will testify. Long-lasting feuds can develop between neighbours simply because one erects a boundary fence two inches the wrong side of an imaginary dividing line. Householders may complain to the police if a motorist leaves a vehicle where they normally park (albeit on a public road). Being on our own patch gives rise to different feelings and attitudes. Most soccer teams win more at home. Liverpool fans started a riot ending in many deaths when Juventus supporters occupied part of 'their' stand. Street gangs may go to great lengths to control certain areas of a city and yet leave others to other groups. The notion of territorial behaviour also has implications on a smaller scale. For example, a police officer interviewing a suspect at their home is at a disadvantage compared to one conducting the same interview at the station (police territory). By the same token, witnesses or victims may benefit from interviews at home.

We hope we have shown in this chapter that a great deal can be learned about people by observation of their non-verbal behaviour. In the same way, we give off non-verbal information to others. The information in both directions is usable. It is not a one-way process.

We must end on some notes of caution. We have assumed responsible use of the awareness of the information in this chapter. Close attention to NVC may well help an investigating officer to elicit a confession from a guilty person. It may also serve to make an innocent person submissive and compliant, interviewed in a strange environment by a person in a position of authority who sits too close for comfort. We hope that officers will be prepared to be convinced by a suspect's non-verbal behaviour – in both directions, innocence as well as guilt. We also wish to emphasize that NVC is an essential component of *all* interactions, not just those involving police officer and suspect. We do not want the reader to form the impression that the interrogation situation is the most important. Members of the public will pay great attention to the police officer's 'attitude', which invariably contains a large non-verbal component.

Finally, police officers should be aware that many of the 'rules' of NVC are *culturally* determined. Therefore people from different cultural backgrounds may behave in ways which should not be interpreted according to the police officer's own background. For example, aversion of eye gaze in some communities is politeness, not shiftiness. Given the fraught nature of many of the relationships between police officers and ethnic community members, it should not be compounded by misunderstandings of NVC display rules.

Review notes

Even when we are not speaking we are communicating non-verbally. To make sense of another person we attend closely to their appearance, though we may be misled through our own use of stereotypes. We can understand interactions by examining the distance between people and the furniture arrangements they use. A person's posture and gestures may tell us a great deal about their mood, attitude and status. Eye contact is an important source of communication and is used to regulate interactions between people. People may behave differently on their own territory compared with when they are on someone else's. Other people are studying your NVC, attempting to understand your moods and attitudes.

References

Bull, R. (1983) Lie detectors don't tell the truth. *Police Review*, 1 July 1983.
Goffman, E. (1956) *The Presentation of Self in Everyday Life*. Edinburgh: Edinburgh University Press.
Hall, E.T. (1966) *The Hidden Dimension*. Garden City, NY: Doubleday.
Inbau, F.E. and Reid, J.F. (1963) *Criminal Interrogation and Confessions*. Toronto: Burns and MacEachern.
Sommer, R. (1969) *Personal Space*. Atlantic City, NJ: Prentice-Hall.
Walkley, J. (1983) Police Interrogation: A study of the psychology, theory and practice of police interrogation and the implications for police training. Unpublished MSc thesis, Cranfield Institute of Technology.
Waltman, J.L. (1983) Non-verbal communication in interrogation: Some applications. *Journal of Police Science and Administration*, 11, 166–169.

Further reading

Argyle, M. (1975) *Bodily Communication*. London: Methuen.
Farrington, D.P. (1981) Psychology and police interrogation. *British Journal of Law and Society*, 18, 97–107.
Sommer, R. (1969) *Personal Space*. Atlantic City, NJ: Prentice Hall.

Chapter 3

Is Seeing Believing?

'I *know* it must be true – I saw it with my own eyes.' How many times have we heard such a statement, only to find some time later that what a person may claim to have 'seen' cannot actually have happened. The witness to the traffic accident or the shopkeeper who has just been robbed will both have a story to tell as to what they saw; or think they saw. We imagine that human vision works more or less like video equipment, the eye being the camera and our memory a video recorder storing information accurately. Unfortunately, this 'common sense' view is wrong. The eyes, ears and other sense organs do 'take in' information from the outside world, but something happens to the information before it is acted upon or stored in our memories. This process is known as *perception* and has been studied extensively by psychologists. We believe it is essential for the police officer to have some understanding of this process so that he or she can make sense of the inaccuracies which creep into the stories of well-intentioned witnesses – including ourselves!

Perception is one of those processes that goes on almost all the time, but in most cases we are unaware of its operation. We are constantly bombarded with information, though we are selective in what we attend to. Whatever enters our sense organs must be *interpreted* before we can react to it and this is what is involved in the process of perception. The words on this page are just black lines on a white background to the eye. Through perception you convert them (we hope) into images, thoughts and information. Our perceptual processes try to impose some kind of structure onto what we see, hear, touch, smell and taste. The sense organ itself does not attach any meaning to what it sees but meaning is imposed by perceptual processes taking place in the brain. In other words, what the eye 'sees' and what the brain 'perceives' may be quite different. Look at the illustration.

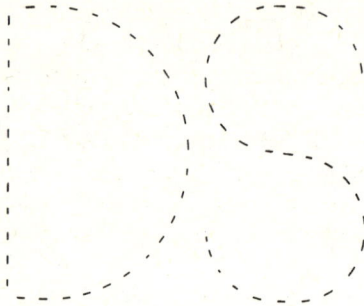

What the eyes see is a collection of dotted lines, but we perceive the letters 'DS'. Note that in order to identify the dots as letters which have some meaning, our perceptual processes have 'filled in' the gaps between the dotted lines so as to make some sense of the pattern. Your perception may even have gone a step further and interpreted the dotted lines as 'Detective Sergeant'!

One of the best ways of illustrating the processes of perception is by reference to the Necker Cube (Figure 3.1).

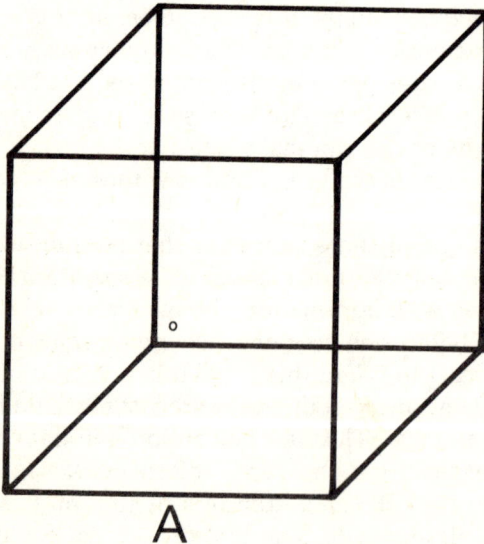

A

Figure 3.1. The Necker Cube.

As you look at the figure it is seen to reverse, Line A sometimes being seen as the front face of the cube, but then appearing to be at the back. Figure 3.1 is in fact a two-dimensional representation. We perceive it to be a representation of a three-dimensional object. We perceive the object to have some depth although it is printed on a flat surface. The reason why the figure appears to reverse is that there are two alternative interpretations of the figure, either one of which could be a correct reading of an (imagined) three-dimensional object. Line A could be at the front of the cube or it could be at the back. Our perception first tests one interpretation and then the other, but can never settle for one option as being more 'accurate' than the other. In other words, our perception actively tests one hypothesis and then the other, but is unable to reach a firm conclusion as to the 'correct' answer. Most objects that we meet in the world are less ambiguous than the Necker Cube, though our perception works in exactly the same way – searching for an interpretation and making 'the best bet' as to what the information represents. In doing this we often attend to the *context* in which we perceive something. Take the example of Figure 3.2.

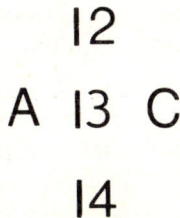

$$12$$

$$A \quad 13 \quad C$$

$$14$$

Figure 3.2.

The middle symbol could be interpreted as a letter B or the number 13, depending on the context. If you cover up the letters A and C, the figure is 'obviously' a 13. If you cover up the 12 and 14, the figure looks more like the letter B.

Our perception is very much influenced by context and all too often we are misled by extraneous information. Let us use estimation of speed as an example of this tendency. We all know how difficult it can be to watch a car going past and accurately estimate its speed. However inaccurate we are though, we may be further confused by certain features of the vehicle. For example, if it is a noisy sports car we may estimate its speed to be greater than if it is an old saloon car. Alfa-Romeo, to name but one manufacturer, uses this fact. It builds in a deliberately growly exhaust note, so that one's sense of its high performance is enhanced. Even the car's colour or the apparent age of the driver may cause us to distort the estimate of speed in certain directions. What happens here is that we add accumulated knowledge to the image of the moving vehicle. We may know from previous experience that sports cars *tend* to go fast – or that young people *tend* to drive faster than old people. We then use this information to help us in interpreting the vehicle's speed. However, this may not always be helpful, as any one particular case may or may not be similar to our previous experience. Though it may be true that young drivers tend to drive faster than older ones, this is not always the case.

The role of expectation

What we believe we have witnessed may often be affected by what we *expect* to see. This is especially the case if we have a limited amount of time to take in the information – for example in a car accident or a handbag snatch. You may wish to try the following exercise to illustrate this point. Figure 3.3 shows a a triangle containing a well-known sentence. Allow yourself *one second only* to look at this, and then write down what you saw. Do this before reading further. Now compare what you wrote with what's actually printed. On the many occasions that we have used this exercise in the classroom (where it is more difficult to cheat!) between 85 per cent and 90 per cent of students do not spot the extra word in the triangle. The figures have been similar for classes of police and prison officers whom the authors have taught for a number of years! You may wish to test your colleagues and friends to confirm this. The reason that many people are fooled in this way is that we often perceive what we *expect* to see.

The sentence 'I love Paris in the spring' is familiar to us and when we have a limited time to take in information (as in this case) we make the 'best bet' as to what our eyes 'saw' – in this instance the best bet was inaccurate. Before dismissing this example as a trick, think of the many instances where a witness has only a split second to take in a mass of information. What he or she expects to see may taint the report of what was seen. This tendency has been demonstrated repeatedly by psychologists. One of the most famous examples was provided by two American researchers almost 40 years ago. Gordon Allport and Leo Postman showed people a picture of a New York subway train filled with people. Most of the figures were seated, but two men were standing. One of the two men was a well-dressed black man and the other was a casually-dressed white man holding an open razor. Each subject viewed the picture briefly and then described it to a second person. The second person told the story to a third and so on until the story had been passed on six times. The researchers then examined the final description given. The most significant finding was that in over half of the experiments using this picture, the final version had the *black* man holding the razor, not the white man. In some cases the black was even said to be threatening the white or brandishing the razor wildly.

Though we know how inaccurate witness statements can be, the distortion that took place here says something about cultural expectations or stereotypes. Subjects could clearly 'see' that the white man held the knife, yet this information was distorted so that it would fit more easily into the subjects' view of the world. The influence of stereotypes is an important factor which is discussed more fully in Chapter 8. However, we would remind the reader that stereotypes significantly affect our perceptions of people – criminals as well as others. Remember that in this particular case people were only shown a picture. Evidence suggests that if people actually see a violent event they take in less detail than if they witness a non-violent event. The main reason for this is that a violent situation is threatening and is thus a source of arousal.

Psychologists have established that too much arousal interferes with many of our abilities, including the capacity to take in information accurately. When under high arousal we tend to narrow our attention to one important feature. For example, a victim of robbery may focus all her attention on the gun the assailant is carrying. Interviewed later she may give a detailed description of the weapon, but no details of the robber.

Personal factors in perception

Perception is essentially a subjective and personal process. Two people may see the same scene but interpret it differently. The known criminal seen entering the church may be perceived by the priest as someone confessing his sins, but perceived by the police officer as about to steal the silver! Many factors affect how and what we perceive, but perception is largely affected by our previous experience and our needs or expectations at the time.

An example of this latter effect was provided in one of the first court cases where a psychologist was called as an expert witness (Sommer, 1959). The case involved a Canadian man who was shot and killed whilst on a hunting trip. The accident occurred partly

Figure 3.3.

because the man was wearing faded red overalls which were more difficult to see in the failing light; but more important was the way in which his companions' 'needs' or 'expectations' led them to define the ambiguous shape as a deer. They were looking for and hoped (or expected) to see a deer, and their perception made the 'best bet' – with tragic consequences. The point is that perception is a valuable tool which helps us to make sense of the world – but it can be misled by many factors. Perhaps anyone else seeing the hunter in red overalls would not have mistaken this ambiguous shape for a deer – but his companions' desire to 'see' a deer led to an incorrect identification of what was perceived.

A great deal of a police officer's day-to-day work will involve keeping eyes and ears open, and accurately – or inaccurately – perceiving people and situations. Courts rely on the testimony of the police officer. Police officers may be seen as experts or more accurate recorders of information than others, but police officers are prone to the same tendencies as others. Whilst an essential part of the officer's training will emphasize the importance of paying attention to detail, other factors may well influence what is noticed. For example, police officers tend to err on the side of suspicion, so that ambiguous incidents are more often interpreted as suspicious, or even as actual offences taking place. This is a consistent finding in experiments both in Britain and America, suggesting that the pressures of police work operate to affect perception in certain identifiable ways.

Obviously a large part of the officer's job will involve looking for the suspicious or unusual, but this searching may lead to inaccurate perceptions of some common behaviours. For example, research by one of us showed that although police officers were no better than civilians at spotting offences contained in a short video tape, police officers tended to be more suspicious of everyday activities taking place (Ainsworth, 1981). Probationer constables were more likely to notice traffic offences than criminal offences, suggesting that their perception was selective. In another experiment a psychologist showed a number of scenes to groups of police officers and civilians. It was reported that the police officers tended to perceive more 'criminal episodes' than the civilians. A man carrying a petrol can was generally perceived as a stranded motorist by the civilians – but was often seen as an arsonist by the police officers.

A similar result was found in another experiment, where groups of police officers and civilians were shown a short film of a man walking up to a pram, pulling down the protective netting and then walking away. At this point a woman came out of a nearby house. Subjects were asked to make a statement about what they saw. They were asked to do this both immediately after the film and a week later. It was found that although the police officers remembered more details about the man's appearance, clothes, etc., they also reported many 'facts' which had not actually occurred. For example, 20 per cent of the police officers reported having seen the man take the baby from the pram – though this did not occur. Similarly, many police officers reported that the woman ran towards the man looking worried. Again this detail was incorrect. What we see here is an example of the process of perception. Police officers *interpreted* what they saw in a certain way. Viewing the man's actions with some suspicion, they made 'the best bet' as to what was going on. When asked to give an account of the incident, the report was a mixture of what was seen and what was assumed to have taken place.

What experiments of this kind show is *not* that police officers are 'worse' or 'better' at perceiving incidents. What they demonstrate is that police officers, like other people, *interpret* events rather than record them like a video camera. It is our belief that if police officers are more aware of the process of perception they are more likely to be accurate in their accounts. Being aware of our own needs, prejudices and expectations tells us all something about how we interpret events and people – and how we remember them.

Visual illusions

One of the ways in which psychologists often demonstrate the process of perception is through the use of visual illusions. We have already seen how a number of internal factors can lead us to perceive things incorrectly, but the same is true of external factors. Although perception is personal and subjective, many people are fooled by certain illusions. Perhaps the best known is the Müller-Lyer illusion (Figure 3.4).

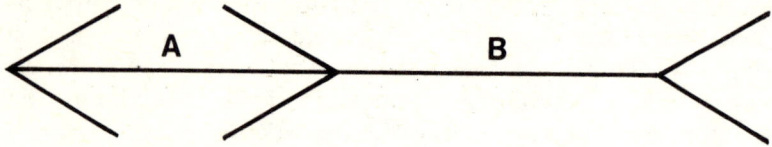

Figure 3.4. The Müller-Lyer Illusion.

Line A appears longer than line B, yet if you measure them with a ruler, you will find they are exactly the same length.

An even more simple illusion is illustrated in Figure 3.5.

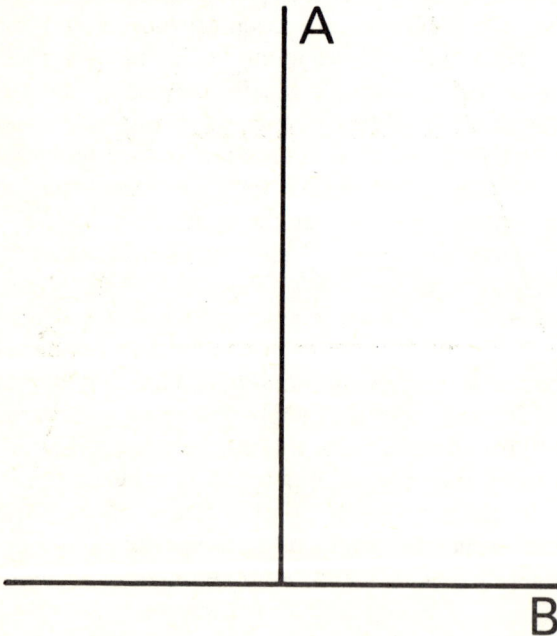

Figure 3.5.

Again line A appears considerably longer than line B, though the two are in fact the same length.

Figure 3.6 shows another example of our not being able to believe our own eyes. The horizontal lines appear to be bowed in the middle though they are in fact straight and parallel.

Figure 3.6.

The problem here is that the lines can only be viewed against their background which we find distracting, or suggestive of lines converging.

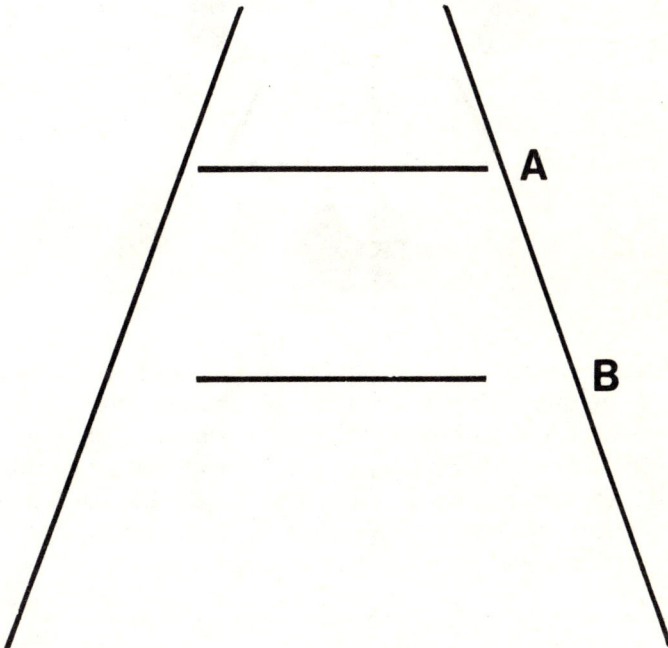

Figure 3.7.

In Figure 3.7 lines A and B are the same length though to most people Line A appears longer. This simple example provides a nice illustration of how our perception relies on previous experience. The two lines which converge towards the top remind us of things going into the distance (for example, railway lines). When we look at railway lines they *appear* to get closer together as they go into the distance. We know from experience though that the train does not fall off the rails, and the converging lines are an illusion created by distance. When we look at Figure 3.7 the converging lines remind us of things going into the distance. We would therefore expect line A to be smaller as it appears 'further away'. We are again relying on previous experience and making assumptions about what we expect to see. This reliance on previous experience can lead us to 'see' things which are not there. The best example is provided in the illusion shown in Figure 3.8.

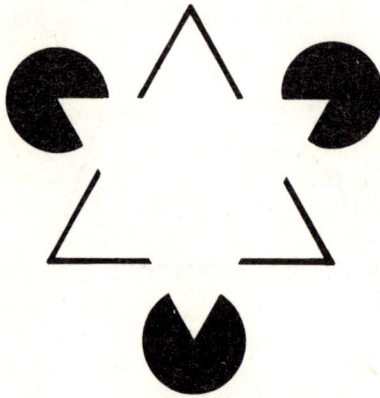

Figure 3.8.

How many triangles do you see in Figure 3.8? Most people see two triangles here, one with a point at the top and one with a point at the bottom. But look carefully at the latter triangle. The lines that make up the sides of the triangle do not, in fact, exist, other than in our minds. Try covering up the three black circles and then spot the lines of the triangle. You will find the triangle mysteriously disappears, only to reappear as soon as you can see the black circles again. What happens here is that your perception fills in the sides of the triangle to try to make sense of the wedges cut out of the circles, and the pieces missing from the other triangle. The best way of making sense of this is to *assume* that there must be a triangle there to make this pattern.

This example of inference shows how difficult it is to report on what is *actually* 'out there' rather than what we assume *should* be there. Any witness testifying in court will inevitably report their inferences as well as what was seen (or heard). They will not be consciously distorting events, but operating in the normal way of making inferences and drawing conclusions from certain information. The trial judge and the jury will similarly make inferences from what they hear and see. Their previous experience will enable them to make inferences about the witness and about the defendant. When we listen to a witness or a defendant giving testimony in court, our opinion of that testimony is inevitably affected by such things as the physical appearance of the person.

Daryl Landy and Elliot Aronson showed how physical attractiveness can significantly affect jurors' opinions of a defendant. In a simulated setting they had jurors choose a sentence for a convicted person. (A normal procedure in American courts.) In some cases, the defendant was an attractive person and in others unattractive. The researchers found that defendants with an attractive character and appearance were sentenced much more leniently than an unattractive defendant (even though the crime committed was exactly the same). If the *victim* was attractive then the defendant received a more severe sentence than if she was unattractive. A similar experiment was carried out where only the physical attractiveness of a female defendant was varied. Again attractiveness had an effect on sentence but in this case attractiveness could be seen to interact with the type of offences committed. For example, if the case was burglary then the attractive defendant received a less severe sentence. On the other hand, if the defendant was accused of an offence involving deception, an attractive woman received a more severe sentence than an unattractive one. It appears as though beauty is something to be admired, but if it is used to assist in the commission of a crime, we are outraged.

Physical attractiveness is a very important component in perception. It has been shown that physically attractive people are assumed to lead more interesting, successful and happy lives. Even naughty acts committed by attractive children are viewed as less serious than the same acts committed by less attractive children. Psychologists have also shown that experienced teachers made higher evaluations of intelligence when a photograph of an attractive (rather than unattractive) child was attached to a school report. This is another example of our stereotyped views of the world. Like the teachers in the last example, police officers may have preconceived notions as to what a certain type of offender *should* look like. Whilst these stereotypes may be helpful in dealing with the complex world, they can blind us to offences committed by people who do not conform to our stereotypes, and thus produce a self-fulfilling prophecy.

Let us take the training of store detectives as an example of how this might occur. The person given the task of training a group of store detectives may believe that the 'typical' shoplifter is a middle-aged woman wearing a heavy overcoat and carrying a large shopping bag. A film may be shown to the trainees with an actor portraying the typical actions of this 'typical' shoplifter. When the store detectives start working the sales floors, their perceptions will be more likely to be focused on the type of person who closely resembles the image provided. If these people come under suspicion, then they are more likely to appear as statistics at the end of the year. Even though it is admitted that a very small proportion of shoplifters are apprehended, those who *are* caught will be considered typical of this class of offender. The ones who do not resemble the stereotype may not come under suspicion and will thus rarely appear in the statistics. In such a way, the training officer will seem to have succeeded in proving that he or she was correct in the description of the 'typical' shoplifter. In fact, this seems a perfect example of the self-fulfilling prophecy.

We have shown in this chapter how all human beings seek, by perception, to make sense of the world. We also hope to have shown that we can all be fooled by ambiguous figures, visual illusions and our own ways of interpretation, and that neither for simple illusions nor for more complex matters of identification are police officers exempt from the general principles of perception, and the distortions which they entail. Perception is the first stage in our memory process and in the next chapter we examine how information, even if perceived accurately, can be distorted in memory.

Review notes

Perception operates largely without us being aware of it. It interprets and makes sense of information we receive from the outside world. We try to make the 'best bet' as to what is actually out there and in some cases we will be wrong. We tend to 'see' what we expect to see, or what we want to see. Visual illusions provide many examples of how our senses can be fooled. Interpretation plays a vital role in perception for police officers, as it does for other people.

References

Ainsworth, P.B. (1981) Incident perception by British police officers. *Law and Human Behaviour*, 5, 231–236.

Allport, G.W. and Postman, L.J. (1949) *The Psychology of Rumor*. New York: Henry Holt.

Landy, D. and Aronson, E. (1960) The influence of the character of the criminal and his victim on the decisions of simulated jurors. *Journal of Experimental Social Psychology*, 5, 141–152.

Sommer, R. (1959) The new look on the witness stand. *Canadian Psychologist*, 8, 94–99.

Further reading

Bull, R. (1979) The influence of stereotypes on person identification. In D.P.Farrington, K. Hawkins and S. Lloyd-Bostock (eds) *Psychology, Law and Legal Process*. London: Macmillan.

Clifford, B.R. and Bull, R. (1978) *The Psychology of Person Identification*. London: Routledge and Kegan Paul.

Gregory, R.L. (1977) *Eye and Brain: The Psychology of Seeing*. London: Weidenfeld and Nicolson.

Yarmey, A.D. (1979) *The Psychology of Eyewitness Testimony*. London: Macmillan.

Chapter 4

Remembering and Forgetting

In the previous chapter we examined how information received by the sense organs is interpreted through the process of *perception*. Much of the information to which we attend is retained in our memory for some future use. Memory is a remarkable resource, allowing us to store massive amounts of information for up to 70 years, or even more. On the other hand we may be frustrated to find that our memory can fail us when we are in the exam room or when we are unable to put a name to a face. Memory has been extensively studied by psychologists for many years and we believe that a number of the research findings have direct relevance to police work.

Perhaps we should start by examining the 'common sense' view of memory. As we mentioned in the previous chapter, to most of us, memory appears to work as a mechanism which accurately records all that occurs in its presence. The criminal justice system helps to sustain this view by trusting a witness to give an account of what actually took place. However, psychologists have known for some time that memory is *not* a literal storage of information. Any piece of information is translated and stored in a shorthand, personalized way. When we are listening to a speech we do not try to memorize every single word – rather we take in the substance of the whole message. When reading this page, your objective is to (try to!) make sense of the words and sentences and pick out the relevant main points. We have seen previously just how important interpretation is for our perception. Our memory stores our *interpretation* of what we have seen or heard but, even then, may distort it so that it fits more readily into our own memory system. This tendency was demonstrated over 50 years ago by Sir Frederic Bartlett (Bartlett, 1932). In one of his experiments he told a short story called 'The War of the Ghosts' to a group of people, and had them recall as much of the story as possible, both immediately afterwards and then some time later. Although the listeners found it impossible to remember every detail contained within the story, of more interest was the way in which the people *translated* the story so that it made better sense to them. The story which Bartlett used was one which would be alien to English people, having been taken from a completely different culture. In order that it could be stored and made available for recall the story had to be connected with something that was already familiar. In this case, the story became more 'conventional', retaining only those characteristics which could be readily assimilated to past experience. The story lost many of its individualizing features. The original phrasing and style was replaced by more current, commonplace expressions.

Bartlett conducted further experiments to see what would happen to the story if it was passed from one person to another, then to another and so on. (This may have been the origin of the game of 'Chinese whispers', or vice versa.) By doing this, he wished to gain an exaggerated form of individual interpretation by having the story filtered through the memories of a number of people. In this case the final version of the story changed very dramatically from the original, having been translated or 'normalized' by a number of different people. We wonder whether the rules which prohibit the admission of hearsay evidence were formulated partly with this sort of process in mind.

The story which a witness may finally produce is influenced by a wide variety of factors which operate at different times:

- at the time of perceiving the incident (learning)
- during the interval between receiving and recall (retention)
- at the time of reconstructing (recall).

Learning

We have considered the influences which might operate at this stage in the previous chapter, so now mention only briefly some of the relevant factors. For example, we have examined how cumulative past experience, present mood and needs all affect interpretation. These factors will determine to some extent which aspects of the incident we attend to and which we assign most importance to.

Retention

The second stage (retention) is the one which we might assume to be the least susceptible to interference. Occasionally we may lose the information, but if and when it is recalled we may assume that what comes out of memory is the same as what went in. However, many factors intervene during the retention period to affect our memory. Perhaps the most obvious reason for memory loss is time. Herman Ebbinghaus demonstrated over 90 years ago that a great deal of what we learn is forgotten within a few hours. Yet despite the many psychological findings of this kind, courts expect witnesses to remember every detail of an incident for up to a year. Though police officers may try to interview witnesses as soon as possible after the incident, some details will still be lost, and the witness tempted to fill in the blanks with what 'must have' happened. Although loss of details over time is well documented, it is far from clear that it is lapse of time itself which is the cause of this. What is much clearer is that memories are changed by *interference* from other memories or new experiences. The 'common sense' view of memory would suggest that any incident would be recorded in its entirety and reproduced in a similar form. Evidence from psychological research suggests that our other accumulated memories can take out, put in or alter details of what is stored.

Let us take an example. A witness sees a car accident where one vehicle skids on a patch of black ice and hits an oncoming car. Shortly after seeing the collision the witness talks to a friend who tells him that the driver of the vehicle which went out of control is an alcoholic and always 'drives like a lunatic'. When later asked for a statement, the witness will give his account which will be inevitably 'tainted' by the more recent information about the driver. The point is that we store any new information about an incident alongside or even on top of existing information and from then on find it difficult to separate the two.

Elizabeth Loftus, a North American psychologist, has studied this phenomenon extensively and her findings warrant detailed attention. Basically, research by Loftus has demonstrated how extraordinarily malleable is a witness' memory. Far from being a permanent record, undisturbed by subsequent events, memory is extremely fragile and can be added to, altered or restructured by something as simple as a leading question or a piece of misleading information. Typical experiments involve showing people a film of a road traffic accident and then asking questions about details of the film. Often the questions deliberately give misleading information, like suggesting the existence of an object that was not actually there. In one early experiment half the people who had just seen a film of a vehicle accident were asked the question 'How fast was the white sports car going when it passed the barn while travelling along the country road?' The first version of the question was deliberately misleading as there was no barn in the film. Despite this, 17 per cent of people in the first group later reported having 'seen' a barn. What seems to have happened here is that the misleading question caused some people to incorporate the non-existent barn into their memory. To put it another way, the false information became integrated into the person's overall memory of the incident. Loftus thus demonstrated that new information can interfere by adding to our memory, but the next step was to establish whether it could also interfere by altering or transforming the memory itself.

To investigate this, Loftus conducted an experiment where people viewed a series of 30 colour slides depicting stages in a car accident. A red Nissan car was seen to approach a junction, turn right and collide with a pedestrian. For half the people a 'Stop' sign was visible at the junction, but for the other half the sign was 'Yield' ('Give Way'). After viewing the slides, people were asked a number of questions, one of which was critical. This concerned another vehicle passing the red Nissan while it was stopped at the junction. Some were asked the question 'Did another car pass the red Nissan while it was stopped at the 'Stop' sign?' For others, the same question was asked, but with the sign described as a 'Yield' sign. The crucial aspect of this experiment was that for half the people the description of the sign contained within the question was accurate, but for the other half it was inaccurate (that is, the 'Stop' sign which they saw was referred to as a 'Yield' sign or vice versa). All the people were later tested to find out if they could identify the sign they had seen in the slides. Of those who had been given the misleading information, 59 per cent incorrectly identified the sign, compared with only 25 per cent of the group who had been given consistent information. This and a number of similar experiments show that presuppositions are capable of transforming memory as well as adding to it.

A more dramatic example of how easily witnesses may be influenced is provided in another Loftus experiment. Before describing this particular experiment let us pause and consider how the police may go about obtaining a witness statement. The first question asked of a witness will typically be 'Can you tell me what happened?' and the witness will describe in his or her own words what was seen (or rather perceived!). Next would come the taking of a statement which the police officer would write down in a standardized format covering relevant details of the incident. The finished product may well contain many more details than were originally present in the brief verbal report of the witness. During the taking of the statement, the police officer will ask a number of questions in order to elicit a more detailed version of the incident. A typical question might be 'How fast were the cars travelling when they hit each other?' Assuming that all parties agree that there was an accident, this would not be considered a leading question as it does not suggest to the witness that the cars were going at any specific speed. Yet, supposing the police officer asked the same question about speed, but used a verb other than 'hit', such as 'bumped', 'collided', 'contacted' or even 'smashed'?

This was exactly the topic which Lofus studied. People were again shown films of car accidents and were asked to judge the speed of the vehicles. All were asked the question, though different verbs were used in asking about the collision. For some groups the word used was 'smashed', for some it was 'hit', and so on. These are the average estimates of speed where different verbs were used in the question:

> 'Contacted' 30.8 mph
> 'Hit' 34 mph
> 'Bumped' 38.1 mph
> 'Collided' 39.3 mph
> 'Smashed' 40.8 mph

Even allowing for the difficulty which witnesses experience in accurately estimating speed, there are large differences in these estimates which are purely the result of the wording of the question. The word 'smashed' may imply or suggest a more severe impact, and thus a greater estimate of speed was given. The wording of any question is obviously crucial and can significantly affect the answer! Even asking 'How *fast* was the vehicle travelling?' may elicit a different answer than 'What speed was the vehicle travelling at?' We must remember at this point that the story a witness tells in court will be an amalgamation of what was seen, and subsequent information about the event. The problem is nicely illustrated by a further Loftus experiment.

Two groups who had seen the same accident were asked immediately afterwards about the speed of the vehicles. For one group the verb used was 'smashed' and for the other it was 'hit'. One week later the witnesses were again interviewed and one of the questions was 'Did you see any broken glass?' There was in fact no broken glass at the scene of the accident. For the witnesses who had been asked the question about the vehicles 'hitting' each other, 14 per cent later reported having 'seen' broken glass; but for those witnesses who had earlier been asked about the speed of the vehicles which 'smashed' into each other, almost a third reported having 'seen' the non-existent broken glass! We can see what has happened here. Witnesses who were asked about the vehicles *smashing* into each other added 'smashed' to their memory of the event. If vehicles 'smash' into each other it is likely that there will be broken glass, and this presumption led many more people to report having 'seen' the glass. We would suggest that if the question had been 'Did you see *the* broken glass?' then even more people would have been tempted to answer affirmatively. Though this form of questioning would be considered 'leading' in the courtroom, the same amount of control would not be exercised by police officers in their attempts to obtain information from a witness. Some ways of 'leading' are quite subtle, and may be used completely unknowingly by the interviewer. For example, the questions 'How far away was the red car?' and 'How close was the red car?' are both legitimate questions designed to gather relevant details – though the different wording may imply different things to a witness. Again, remember that once the answer is given, it will be incorporated into the overall memory of the episode.

The subtlety of influence may even be considered to extend to the non-verbal cues which an interviewing officer may 'give off' (see Chapter 2). A quizzical glance may tell the witness that his or her story is considered dubious, whereas a nod of approval may help to confirm that the witness's story is approved of. Of course, the actual *writing* of witness statements is a further source of distortion. Here, the witness may be aided by an officer in phrasing the statement. The witness's memory is influenced both by the questions the officer poses and the way in which he or she phrases the statement afterwards. In both these ways, the witness's actual memory comes closer to the image the police officer has of an accident.

Memory for faces. Attempts by police officers to obtain accurate descriptions of a suspect must also be considered here. When seeing someone for the first time we form an impression of them. We rarely consider individual details such as eye colour, shape of nose, etc., though these details will generally be asked for by the investigating officer. (Can you remember your mother's eye colour?) A witness may well give all the information he or she can, and then later be asked to try to identify the suspect from an ID parade. Bearing in mind the research, the witness will be looking for a face which both resembles what was seen earlier and fits in with any new information. We may like to think that memory for faces is different from memory of an accident. The terrified witness may well proclaim 'I'll never forget that face as long as I live' and later fail to pick out the prime suspect on the ID parade. This, self-evidently, may be because the suspect is innocent or because of memory failure. We discuss the problems of ID parades in more detail later, but for the present let us consider whether interference may affect memory for faces, in the same way as it does memory for incidents.

We turn again to research conducted by Elizabeth Loftus. In a series of experiments, subjects saw an individual, either in a photograph, a film or live. Subsequently, some subjects were exposed to misleading information, either by hearing a description supposedly given by another witness or by being asked a misleading question. If witnesses heard a second 'witness' referring to a misleading feature (for example, a moustache), over a third of the genuine witnesses later included this (false) detail in their own description, often using the exact wording used by the misleading witness. More worrying though, was the fact that of the witnesses exposed to another's description, 70 per cent later 'recognized' an individual whose face contained the false feature referred to. If the witness heard another person say the suspect had a moustache, 70 per cent of the original witnesses later picked out a face sporting a moustache – this despite the fact that the face they had seen did not have a moustache. Similarly, if witnesses were asked leading questions containing misinformation about a critical feature (a moustache) almost a third later said they had 'seen' the moustache on the face.

These results support the view that memory for faces can be affected by the introduction of misleading information, in the same way as memory for events. The skill of police interviewers is thus very important, if they are to avoid putting words into the mouths of witnesses. We have seen how easily witnesses pick up the verbal expressions which others use, and incorporate these into their memory of the face.

One final point about misleading information concerns its timing. Much of the research has shown that misleading information is most effective when it is given some time after the witness has seen the incident. Whilst accepting the practical difficulties of obtaining witness statements immediately after an incident, doing so would mean that the witness will be less readily influenced by erroneous information than if interviewed a week later.

Recall

We have examined in the previous pages some of the factors which can influence memory at the *recording* and *retention* stages, but equally important are the influences which may operate at the time of *recall*. The most obvious factor to be considered here is *stress* (see Chapter 12). Stress affects the amount of information which is taken in. It is also true that high levels of stress will affect both the amount and the accuracy of information *retrieved* from memory. Most of us will have experienced the trauma of the examination room where it seems much more difficult to recall information that was well rehearsed even the previous day. The examination room is an ideal stress-inducing environment. We are there to be tested or assessed, and this reflects heavily on our self-image ('I must not fail'). The examination room is also 'threatening' in the sense that it is a strange and novel environment and, therefore, one to which we rarely adapt.

Psychologists have established that human beings function best within an optimum range of stimulation or stress. Too little stimulation and we are bored or may even fall asleep, too much arousal and our performance begins to be affected in many ways. Whilst it has been established that people with a generally high level of anxiety make less accurate witnesses, it is also true that stress-inducing situations interfere with accurate recall. Let us consider the witness giving evidence in court. Just like the student in the exam room, he or she is under pressure to 'do their best' or perform well, and in a situation which is novel and unrehearsed. Those readers who are experienced police officers may wish to try to recall their feelings the first time they had to give evidence – and compare this with feelings experienced when the task was much more familiar. Nevertheless, courts rarely even attempt to make witnesses feel more relaxed, expecting them simply to be accurate 'memory machines'.

The issue of *where* the information is recalled is equally important for the police officer taking a witness statement. Over 40 years ago, Edward Abernathy demonstrated that students performed much worse on their examinations if tests were administered in a different room from that where the teaching was carried out. From this, and more recent psychological evidence, it would seem that accurate recall would be more likely if witnesses were taken back to the scene of the incident and interviewed there, rather than the prevalent practice of obtaining statements at the police station. Whilst recognizing that it is beset with obvious practical difficulties, we wonder if witnesses would perform more accurately at ID parades if these took place at the scene of the crime, rather than at the police station. Returning to the scene may well provide the witness with a larger number of reminders, so that he or she can recall more information. A variation of this approach is now being used with reconstructions of a murder victim's last movements. The hope is that this reconstruction will jog a person's memory and provide new clues. Whilst applauding this innovation we would caution investigators that a witness will come forward with information which may be an amalgamation of what was originally seen and what was shown in the reconstruction. Similarly, television programmes such as *Crimewatch UK* may serve to jog memories but may also give a witness new information which is then joined with their original memory of the incident. When giving evidence later, a witness may find it difficult to differentiate between the original memory and the subsequent information provided by the television programme.

Just like the courtroom or examination room, the identification parade can be stressful. The situation will be strange and unrehearsed for most witnesses. Their attendance will force them to relive what will probably have been an extremely traumatic event. In addition they know that they may be face to face with 'their' offender. Police officers often despair when a witness fails to pick out the suspect. We would suggest that stress plays a significant role in non-identification. Recent resarch (Ainsworth and King) found that witnesses who admitted being nervous were much less likely to pick out the suspect than witnesses who did not feel nervous. Similarly, those witnesses who admitted fearing recriminations were much less likely to identify a suspect. The rules governing the conduct of ID parades are designed to ensure fairness, but give little guidance on how to reduce the stress which is inevitably felt by the witness. For example, use of a one-way screen is commonplace in America, though not found in England at the time of writing. The advantage of this system is obvious: the witness will feel less stress if he or she knows that the suspect cannot see them. Of the witnesses who were interviewed in the study by Ainsworth and King some 79 per cent thought that one-way screens would be a distinct advantage, helping to reduce any feelings of intimidation. Over half the witnesses also thought that some 'notes of guidance' would be helpful in preparing them for the task in hand. Ray Bull also suggests that parading those on display one at a time past the witness (who does not know how many people are in the parade) would increase the proportion of accurate identifications.

Hypnosis

There has been a great deal of discussion recently about the use of hypnosis on crime witnesses. It has been suggested that under hypnosis a witness or a suspect will recall more details of an incident and also be more accurate. The issue has produced furious disagreement amongst laypersons and academics alike.

Hypnosis was used by psychologists many years ago to uncover 'lost' memories. It was used to discover desires and motives long since buried. More recently hypnosis has been used as a form of therapy for people who have undergone a particularly traumatic experience. The therapist is able to take the patient back over the event and allow him or her to work through the feelings generated.

Most recently, interest has focused on attempts to gain information from witnesses and suspects while under hypnosis. Early reports on this, especially in the USA, seemed to show that witnesses were able to remember more details of an incident whilst under hypnosis than when originally interviewed. The major problem with the technique is that under hypnosis a witness may be even more 'suggestible' than when in a 'normal' state of consciousness. We have seen earlier in the chapter just how easy it is to influence a witness's account under normal circumstances. The problem seems even more acute when a witness is under hypnosis. There have been some celebrated cases where people have been convicted on the basis of information supplied by a hypnotized witness, but that is no guarantee of its accuracy. There are documented cases where information given by a witness under hypnosis has been proved to be totally inaccurate! The problem of suggestibility has recently led to a ruling in the USA that a witness who has been interrogated under hypnosis cannot later be called on to give evidence in court. The reasoning behind this is that their subsequent testimony is likely to have been 'tainted' by the questioning under hypnosis.

Our view is that though hypnosis undoubtedly can on occasion improve *access* to memories it cannot necessarily improve the *accuracy* of the memory. In other words a hypnotized witness will generally give more information about an incident – but that information is not likely to be of any better quality. Not only may witnesses provide unhelpful information spontaneously, but the hypnotic state does not protect them from the errors of perception and memory we have already described. While debate continues over the use of hypnosis, we feel that police officers should be made aware of the dangers inherent in the technique, and the interested reader may wish to pursue some of the references at the end of this chapter.

We have shown that memory, like perception, is not just like a machine to replay a memory tape, which stands unchanged for all time. Any memory is subject to a whole series of influences which can affect the final reconstruction. While the criminal justice system continues to place such importance on eyewitness testimony we believe it vital that police officers be made aware of the possible sources of distortion – and then to use the techniques of interrogation which are least likely to distort an original memory. We also hope that the reader will be aware that his or her own memory is easily influenced in the same way as that of civilians!

Review notes

Memory does not simply record and replay accurate details of every event we witness. Interpretation plays a vital role and may introduce distortions. Memory can be distorted by factors operating at the time of learning, during the retention period, and at the time of recall. Research has shown that memory can easily be changed by subsequent information or misinformation about an incident and by the turn of phrase used by an interviewer. Even memory for faces can be affected by subsequent misleading information. Stress can interfere with accurate recall, yet the criminal justice system does little to reduce the stress which a witness may be experiencing. Hypnosis can be used to aid recall by improving access to a memory. It does not increase the accuracy of the memory itself.

References

Ainsworth, P.B. and King, E. Witness perceptions of identfication parades. (Unpublished paper available from the first author.)
Bartlett, F.E. (1932) *Remembering: A study in experimental and social psychology.* Cambridge: Cambridge University Press.
Loftus, E.F. and Greene, E. (1980) Warning: Even memory for faces may be contagious. *Law and Human Behaviour 4,* 322-334.

Further reading

Clifford, B.R. and Bull, R. (1978) *The Psychology of Person Identification.* London: Routledge and Kegan Paul.
Farrington, D.P., Hawkins, K. and Lloyd-Bostock, S. (eds) (1979) *Psychology, Law and Legal Processes.* London: Macmillan.
Lloyd-Bostock, S.M.A. (ed.) (1981) *Psychology in Legal Contexts: Applications and Limitations.* London: Macmillan.
Loftus, E.F. (1979) *Eyewitness Memory.* Cambridge, Mass.: Harvard University Press.

Shepherd, J.W., Ellis H.D. and Davies, G.M. (1982) *Identification Evidence: A Psychological Evaluation.* Aberdeen: Aberdeen University Press.
Lloyd-Bostock, S.M.A. and Clifford, B.R. (1983) *Evaluating Witness Evidence.* Chichester: Wiley.

Chapter 5

To Help or Not to Help

There is safety in numbers – or so we are told. The presence of large numbers of other people reassures us that we are safe. If anything should happen to us, we know that people would come to our aid. Police officers are entitled to call upon assistance from the public in certain situations when the failure to help can lead to criminal proceedings. The streets appear much safer when we are surrounded by our fellow citizens. The street deserted but for a single stranger lurking in the shadows is the stuff of which many a good suspense thriller is made. Yet this common assumption of security in crowded places may be ill founded.

All too often police officers or ambulance personnel attend incidents where many people are gazing with an almost morbid fascination – yet no one is doing anything 'positive'. Perhaps the most notorious case of this kind occurred in New York City in 1964 and involved a woman called Kitty Genovese. She was 32 years old. One night she left the bar where she had been working and walked home. As she neared her apartment block she was attacked, assaulted and eventually died of multiple stab wounds. The event itself was horrific. However, the facts surrounding the case are even more disturbing. Kitty did not die suddenly, unseen by anyone. Far from it. Her assailant took 30 minutes to kill her, during which time she screamed and pleaded for help. Her cries certainly did not go unnoticed. It was later established that some 38 people witnessed the crime, yet no one intervened, nor did anyone contact the police.

The incident became the journalistic sensation of the year, and the media speculated on how such a thing could be allowed to happen. Accusations of 'apathy' and 'moral callousness' were made, and the case was cited as a glaring example of the decline of 'civilization' in the city. Though the British reader may have an image of New

York City as being a place where 'this sort of thing happens all the time', we cannot dismiss the case as irrelevant to us. Research by psychologists suggests that the explanations offered at the time may be neither helpful nor accurate. Whilst much has been written about the dehumanizing effects of city life (see Chapter 7), simple callousness cannot explain the unusual behaviour of the witnesses. The 38 people did not merely look at the scene once and then ignore it. They watched, apparently fascinated. Many later admitted to having been disturbed by what they saw, yet they stared on. They were unwilling to help yet seemed unable to turn away. This behaviour was not heroic, but neither was it indifferent, nor apathetic. In fact it was like crowd behaviour in many situations with which the police may have to deal. A road accident, a fire or a collapse in the street all seem to attract large crowds which look on in helpless fascination – but without getting involved directly. Can this behaviour be explained away as indifference or alienation? We think not. These same people would undoubtedly be willing to help a stranger if they were asked for directions to the local hospital – yet ironically the same stranger might receive less assistance if she collapsed to the ground clutching her chest and frothing at the mouth. The reason is that the latter case represents an emergency and the very nature of an emergency implies certain psychological consequences. Bibb Latané and John Darley list five characteristics which make an emergency distinctive.

1. *It involves threat or harm.* Invariably property, well being or even life will be in danger. The house fire may not only claim the lives of its occupants, but also the life of the would-be rescuer. This, coupled with the fact that the rewards for intervention are negligible, means that there are psychological pressures on any individual to ignore a possible emergency. The reluctant hero may use a more subtle mechanism, however – distorting his or her perception of it or underestimating his or her responsibility for coping with it.

2. *It is an unusual or rare event.* Whilst experienced police officers may accumulate relevant experience and receive appropriate training in dealing with emergencies, the average person will have little direct experience. Psychologists often note how a great deal of our everyday behaviour is guided by familiar and stereotyped 'patterns'. The rare 'emergency' represents a novel situation for which most people are untrained and unprepared.

3. *Emergencies differ widely, one from another.* Whilst many emer-

gencies share *some* common characteristics, knowledge specific to one type may be irrelevant to another. There are, for example, few features common to a robbery, a fire and a car accident. Our culture provides the non-specialist with little relevant know-how. Whilst *generalized* advice may be freely available, it is typically inadequate or inappropriate for a *specific* emergency situation.

4. *Emergencies are unforeseen.* The police officer summoned to an incident will have some notion of what the incident involves. He or she will know if the ambulance or fire service is attending, and will have some time to rehearse the probable procedures. The person in the street who first notices an event must decide on a course of action *without* the benefit of forethought and planning. Also, he or she will not have the benefits of a personal radio to consult others on the best course of action or summon others who may be better equipped to deal with the problem.

5. *Emergencies require instant action.* In most cases, unless it is dealt with immediately, the situation will deteriorate. The fire may spread, more vehicles may crash into the accident wreckage, the drowning child may go under for a third time. Whatever the emergency, there are urgent pressures to deal with the situation at once, and the individual is placed under considerable stress. There is rarely time to weigh up alternative courses of action.

Given these considerations, the non-intervention of a bystander is perhaps more understandable. Even if an individual does decide to intervene, he or she will have gone through a number of identifiable processes.

First, and perhaps most obviously, the person must notice that something is happening. Whilst the police officer may be constantly looking for the unusual, the person in the street may be deep in his or her own thoughts and simply fail to notice an event. It has been found, however, that many people who do not offer help or assistance may later seek to justify their non-intervention by denying any knowledge of it. We discuss this point later in more detail.

Not only must the bystander notice an event, but he or she must *interpret* it correctly. 'Could that really be a gunshot? Probably just a car backfiring.' 'Is that really a woman screaming? No, I'm sure it's just children playing.' How often have police officers interviewed neighbours or witnesses and listened in amazement to their incredible interpretation of what the police already knew to be a serious incident? For many years the public have been told 'If you see some thing suspicious, dial 999.' The problem has always been one of *interpretation*. Whilst the police officer's suspicions may be easily aroused, the general public is largely unaccustomed to the sounds of people in trouble, or an emergency.

In Chapter 3, we examined the topics of 'perception' and 'interpretation'. It may be appropriate to mention the subject again at this point. Our senses (sight, hearing, etc.) receive information from the outside world. This information is then *interpreted* according to a number of different criteria. Our attempts to 'make sense' of the information are largely based on our previous relevant experience. If the information is novel and vague, then we may well reach an incorrect conclusion. The person in the street may never before have heard a gunshot, so his or her attempt to make sense of this noise may well result in it being incorrectly perceived or interpreted. The topic of perception is important if we are to understand why people behave the way they do. For the present, we would merely wish to draw the reader's attention to the point made in Chapter 3 that interpretation is a vital feature of perception and is inevitably subjective.

Even if the witness correctly interprets the event, he or she will still have to decide whether it is his or her responsibility to take some action. Perhaps some other witness is more qualified. Rarely would a witness to an accident be more relieved than to hear the words 'It's all right, stand back, I'm a police officer.'

If someone assumes the responsibility to do something, his or her course of action is still uncertain. A decision must be reached as to what form of assistance is the most appropriate. Should the person rush in and directly offer to help – or should he or she detour to call a doctor or the police? Finally, the helpful person must decide how to implement his or her choice of action. Where is the nearest telephone? What is the quickest way to the hospital? Only at this point may the person actually begin to act.

In offering this model, Latané and Darley acknowledge that it is perhaps too rational. The panicky bystander will be unlikely to go through these decisions in a logical order. Indeed he or she may well vacillate between a number of options and even try various strategies before finally being committed to one course of action. It should also be noted that the bystander is not a detached and objective observer. His or her actions have personal consequences as well as affecting the victim. He or she may be left with a sense of pride or even become a hero. Conversely, the 'would-be' helper may be embarrassed, sued or physically harmed.

The influence of others

Perhaps the most crucial factor affecting the bystander's choice, however, is the decision that he or she perceives *other* bystanders to be making. If the 50 other people walking along the street ignore the collapsed woman, then the individual will take this as an indication that the incident is not serious, and the 'appropriate' course of action is non-intervention. In other words the consensus will strongly affect the perceptions of each passer-by and discourage intervention. The individual could discuss the incident with his or her fellow citizens, but, more likely, attitudes will be *inferred* from behaviour. If the inferences are correct, we would expect there to be a consensus of opinion as to the appropriate response. However, we cannot assume that all passers-by will be exhibiting their true feelings. Whilst it is undoubtedly true that each member of a group of bystanders may watch others' reactions, the individual is also aware of being watched by others. Among males especially it could be considered desirable to appear calm and collected even in times of stress. In other words, the individual under scrutiny from other people is *less* likely to react in case it turns out that he or she has *over*-reacted and thus is embarrassed or ridiculed. The bystander may be genuinely concerned for the apparent victim, but when under public gaze may still maintain an unconcerned air.

The dangers of this reaction are obvious: if each potential 'Good Samaritan' is trying to appear calm, but is simultaneously gauging the reactions of others, then all present may be led to label the situation incorrectly. In other words each individual will be influenced by every other individual and the cool exteriors will lead to the situation being defined as *less* serious than it really is. Latané and Darley refer to this as 'a state of pluralistic ignorance'. The end point of this reasoning is that an individual is *less* likely to intervene in an emergency if others are present than if he or she is the sole bystander. This conflicts somewhat with the notion of 'safety in numbers', and leads us to question the security which we feel when surrounded by large numbers of others.

As you will read throughout this book (and contrary to the impression you would get from just reading the popular press), psychologists do not simply devise a theory and leave it at that. In fact Latané and Darley set out to test the accuracy of their theories in a number of controlled experiments both inside and outside the laboratory.

Testing bystander apathy

The first experiment set out to test whether there would be any differences in the responses of a group of students to a potential emergency, depending on whether they were alone or with other people. The students who took part in the study were not told the true nature of the experiment, but were asked to fill out a questionnaire in a small room. Whilst they were doing this, smoke started to pour into the room from a wall vent. The students were observed to see whether they reacted to the emergency by telling the experimenter of the smoke. The crucial variable introduced into the experiment was that some were alone in the room (Condition 1), some were in groups of three (Condition 2), and in the third condition a student shared a room with two confederates of the experimenter. The confederates had been specifically instructed not to react to the smoke, but to carry on with their task as if there was no problem. The experiment lasted for six minutes, after which the smoke was stopped and the students were told the true nature of the experiment.

Of the students who were alone in the room when the smoke was introduced, some 75 per cent reported the potential danger to the experimenter. This contrasts sharply with Condition 3 where only 10 per cent reported the smoke. So the actions of the two 'stooges' who had been instructed to behave in a certain way significantly affected the reactions of the third person. But what about Condition 2? Remember that in this case all three students were not expecting the smoke and, one might have thought, would have reacted similarly to those who were alone in the room. In fact their reactions were very different, with only 15 per cent taking any action. This was despite the fact that towards the end of the six-minute period the smoke was so dense that they had difficulty seeing the questionnaire they were supposed to be completing!

When later questioned about their reactions, the students who had not reported the smoke gave a variety of explanations. They generally explained their behaviour by claiming that they considered the smoke not to be a danger. Some thought it might be steam, some even claiming it might be a 'truth gas'! Whether these are *actual* reasons or merely justifications for inaction it is difficult to say. Human beings have a tendency to justify their behaviour, no matter how implausible the feedback may appear to the observer (see Chapter 6). In this experiment, the subjects who were with others cast frequent glances around the room, to see if others were reacting. They appeared to 'define the situation' by watching the reactions of others who were also watching them and waiting for *them* to react. Interestingly, 80 per cent of the people who did intervene did so during the first three minutes. In other words, the longer the experiment went on, the less likely it was that people would react – this despite the fact that the smoke got steadily worse. It was as if they were reluctant to change a decision made early on, despite the worsening situation.

Another interesting aspect of the case was the fact that when interviewed later, people largely claimed that their decision was *not* influenced by the reactions of the other people in the room. The results demonstrate that the presence of others did have dramatic effects on behaviour, and yet those affected were either unaware of this or refused to acknowledge that they were influenced by others. This finding is common to many social psychological investigations which are discussed in Chapter 6.

This relatively simple experiment does seem to support Latané and Darley's theory as to the inhibiting effect of the presence of other people, though the results could to some extent be explained by the fact that the smoke may have been perceived as a threat. It could be that the people who were in groups of three may have felt less threatened by a possible fire, as they considered three people would be better able to deal with the situation than one. They may also have been motivated to hide their own fear from others and appear brave and unconcerned. In order to examine this possibility, a second experiment was carried out using a situation which did not involve a personal threat to the individual.

This second experiment again involved American male students who volunteered to help with what was supposedly a market research study. Whilst filling in a questionnaire they heard the sound of a woman apparently falling off a chair and injuring herself. They could choose to go to the woman's assistance or ignore the event, and again the main focus of interest was whether the presence of other people would significantly affect the decision to offer help. Some of those studied were alone in a room adjacent to where the fall had taken place – others had a partner. In some cases the 'partner' was a fellow student, but in other cases (as you may have guessed) the second person was a confederate of the experimenter, who was instructed to ignore the cries for help emanating from the adjacent room. In fact, a further variation was introduced in that the two students waiting together were in some cases unknown to each other and in other cases were friends who had come along together.

The results of this experiment are thought-provoking. When subjects were alone hearing the woman in distress, some 70 per cent went to her assistance. This contrasts sharply with the results for those who shared the room with a non-reacting confederate. In this case only some 7 per cent offered help. When the two naïve people were unknown to each other, only 23 per cent offered help, though when friends were in the room together, 45 per cent went to try and help. You will notice that even when the two people were friends the woman was still less likely to be helped than if only one person was present. When the two people present were friends, they often discussed the apparent accident and then intervened. When the two were unknown to each other, they rarely discussed what they had heard.

None of the people who failed to intervene considered their inaction to be callous or apathetic, but provided a number of different reasons – or justifications – for non-intervention. Some even explained their non-involvement in terms of *concern* for the victim – they said they did not wish to embarrass her! Those who had not gone to the woman's assistance invariably claimed that in a 'real' emergency they would be among the first to help. Again in this experiment non-interveners rarely admitted to being influenced by the presence of another person – though the results clearly demonstrate that this was the case. We should also note that the presence of only one fellow witness produced similar results to the presence of two others in the previous experiment. This situation represented no personal danger to the would-be helpers, yet the results are largely similar to those from the first experiment. We cannot therefore explain the results of the first experiment simply in terms of the 'safety in numbers' idea.

Many other experiments of the same general type have been carried out and the results are always similar – the *more* people who witness an emergency situation, the *less* likely it is that action will be taken by any particular individual. The sceptical reader may seek to diminish the value of many of the findings in view of the fact that the experiments were carried out in the psychology laboratory. It could be suggested that people entering a psychology laboratory may be already suspicious of the procedures employed and thus behave in an 'abnormal' way.

In an effort to dispel this suggestion, Bibb Latané and his colleague Donald Elman carried out an experiment not in a laboratory but in a liquor store (off-licence) in the USA. The basic procedure of the experiment involved either one or two people apparently stealing a case of beer. In fact this was specially set up, though people who witnessed the 'crime' had no notion that their actions were under scrutiny. The procedure employed was that the 'thief' would enter the store, either alone or with an accomplice, and ask the shopkeeper about a particular type of beer. While the shopkeeper was in a back room, the thief picked up a case of beer, saying 'They'll never miss this' and left the store without attempting to pay for the goods. In total, this procedure was carried out 96 times over a two-week period. On exactly half the occasions there was one 'thief' involved, and on the other half two.

In line with the previous experiments, the reseachers were particularly interested in establishing whether there was any difference if the 'emergency' was witnessed by only one person compared with when it was viewed by more than one. Thus in 48 of the 96 'thefts' there was one other person present, and on the other occasions there were two people at the counter. The theft itself took less than a minute, and the apparent thieves are described as 'husky young men'. Perhaps for these reasons, none of the witnesses tried directly to prevent the theft. They could, however, inform the shopkeeper of what they had seen when he returned to the counter, and some 20 per cent of the witnesses did this. If nothing was said then the shopkeeper asked what had happened to the man or men who had been there earlier. Just over half of the remaining witnesses did report what they had seen under this prompting.

One reason for the low rate of reporting could well have been the witnesses' fear of retaliation from the criminals. Yet if this were the explanation we might expect there to be more fear if there were two thieves than if there was only one. In fact the theft was more often reported when committed by two people. This difference was thus in the opposite direction from what you might have expected. If fear of reprisal was the main consideration, then we might expect the female to be more fearful than the male witnesses. The results of the experiment actually showed that females were just as likely to report the theft as were the males. The main result however was in line with all the previous laboratory studies mentioned. When a person witnessed an incident alone, he or she was much more likely to take some action (in this case report the theft) than when someone else was present. This particular experiment was carried out away from the psychology laboratory and with people who had no reason to believe that they were being studied, yet it still produced results which support the basic notion, that the more people who witness an event, the less likely it is that any one person will intervene.

Think back to the Kitty Genovese case and the 38 witnesses. An extreme view might be that Kitty was 38 times *more* likely to be helped than if only one person saw what was happening. In fact the large number of witnesses would actually diminish the chances that any one person would help. There was obviously a certain amount of diffusion of responsibility, but also it seems likely that a state of 'pluralistic ignorance' would develop with everyone trying to appear calm – and being fooled by everyone else doing the same. All the experiments have provided examples of people whose actions are significantly affected by the presence of others – whether they are aware of it or not (see Chapter 6).

While it is true that some people are more helpful and altruistic than others, Latané and Darley were unable to find any personality variables which differentiated between helpers and non-helpers. For example, following one experiment where subjects had the opportunity to assist someone who had apparently suffered a seizure, personality tests were administered to all participants. The tests included measures of 'Social Responsibility', 'Need for Approval' and 'Authoritarian Personality'. Although all the tests used were approved and validated measures, which had been shown to be associated with behaviour, none of them predicted helping behaviour in this instance. One reason for this may be that personality characteristics may produce conflicting responses. For example, the kind-hearted, helpful individual may be too frightened to help. The brave and stoic person may actually be rather unconcerned when 'weaker' people need help. Similarly, relevant personality characteristics may influence behaviour in one situation but not in another. The overwhelming conclusion is summarized by Latané and Darley thus:

> The explanation of bystander 'apathy' may lie more in the bystander's response to other observers than in presumed personality deficiencies of 'apathetic' individuals.

With the failure of these personality tests to explain differences in behaviour, the researchers examined some demographic variables of the individuals. For example, people were asked about their social class, how many brothers and sisters they had, their age, whether they were regular church attenders, etc. One of the only two variables which showed any significant result was the size of the community in which the person grew up – the smaller the size of the community in which they were raised, the more likely they were to help. The other variable which appeared significant was the person's social class. Initially it was suggested that lower-middle-class people were quicker to help than upper-middle-class people. Subsequent investigations of this result showed that it was not so much social class as familiarity with the surroundings in which the incident occurred. For example, when incidents were staged at an airport or on a subway station, the apparent victim was more likely to receive help from people to whom the environment was familiar. Similarly, a person is more likely to intervene if the *situation* is not totally unfamiliar. One psychologist interviewed a sample of individuals who had intervened in crimes (mainly robberies) and compared them with a sample of people who had failed to intervene. The major difference between the groups was that the interveners were more competent to deal with the event: that is, they had some form of training that involved dealing with emergencies. They were also on average taller and heavier and described themselves as strong or aggressive!

Despite these helpful findings, it remains extremely difficult to predict if particular people (even ourselves) would or would not help in a specific situation. Whilst few of us would admit to being callous or capable of ignoring the distress of a fellow human being, situational forces often make people behave unpredictably. But, if we are made aware of the situational pressures which we are all under, it may be possible to overcome the pressures towards inaction in a more altruistic way. Latané and Darley do *not* take the view that urban life has permanently changed the attitudes of the inhabitants of the city to the point where victims like Kitty Genovese can be ignored without a second thought. Rather the city may have made us more susceptible to social influence and to a fear of embarrassment and ridicule if we intervene ineffectively. Recent research on the 'altruistic personality' suggests that some individuals are more likely to offer help than others across a variety of situations, but prediction of behaviour in one specific situation is difficult if based purely on personality descriptions.

One notion that we have not considered so far is that certain people or categories of people may be more likely to *receive* help than others. The old lady who falls in the street may be more likely to be helped than the youth who trips. This notion has been tested by a number of psychologists, though we would wish to draw particular attention to experiments carried out by two British psychologists, David Farrington and Barrie Knight. Their experiments involved a variant of the so-called 'lost letter' technique. Stamped, addressed, unsealed, apparently lost letters, each containing a hand-written note and an amount of money were dropped on the streets of London and picked up by members of the public. The main interest of the studies was whether the letter and its contents were returned intact to the intended recipient.

In the first set of experiments, the victim was made to appear as either an upper-class man sending money for a yachting magazine, or an old lady receiving a refund from a senior citizens' outing. The amounts of money were the same. Although many variables were studied there was a significant difference in the number of letters returned depending upon who the victim was. In the case of envelopes containing cash, less than a quarter of those sent out by the male yachtsman were returned, compared with four-fifths of those addressed to the female old-age-pensioner. Whilst experiments of this kind raise a large number of ethical questions (for instance, whether the psychologists were in effect encouraging people to steal), they provide insights into the circumstances under which people are helpful or non-helpful. They also suggest that we would be naïve to label people as either honest or dishonest, the circumstances having a considerable influence on people's behaviour.

By drawing people's attention to the situational pressures we may also succeed in making people aware of the potential dangers of 'pluralistic ignorance'. A celebrated case in point is that of a female college student who, after hearing of Latané and Darley's work, successfully raised the alarm on discovering a fire, rather than simply assuming that someone else would do so. The numerous witnesses to the Kitty Genovese murder also became more determined to act in future incidents, leading in one case to the arrest of a murderer.

Some practical applications

We have shown in this chapter that not all people who fail to intervene in an emergency do so because they are callous or uncaring. We have seen just how powerful can be the influence of other people (a theme to which we return in the next chapter). We hope that after reading this chapter, police officers will have more insight into the processes involved in deciding whether to help someone. The implications for police work should be obvious: members of the public are more likely to help if they feel personally responsible for an outcome. Neighbourhood Watch schemes may be more successful if small numbers of people are given responsibility, rather than allowing a diffusion of responsibility among a large number of citizens. Police officers requiring assistance (for example, when arresting someone) may be more likely to succeed in getting help if they ask a *particular* individual in the crowd to help, rather than addressing their request to the group at large.

The police rely heavily on the public for help in their job. Appeals to the public should stress that the responsibility lies on the person addressed. Perhaps that is why the World War I poster 'Your country needs you' was so powerful – Lord Kitchener's finger was pointing straight at the person reading it. People should be told not to wait for someone else to do something. Police officers lecturing to members of the public may wish to tell the Kitty Genovese story to audiences as a reminder of the dangers of passing the buck and not picking up the phone and ringing the police. Police officers should also be aware that their own actions will be affected by the presence of a large number of colleagues at any incident.

Review notes

The presence of a large number of other people is no guarantee of safety. In fact, psychological research has shown that the more people who witness an emergency, the less likely it is that any one of them will intervene. Failing to act is typically not the result of callousness or apathy, but a function of groups inhibiting the behaviour of individuals. People look to others for help in defining an ambiguous situation, but if everyone tries to appear calm and unconcerned, a state of 'pluralistic ignorance' develops. An examination of the exact nature of emergencies is necessary if we are to understand the pressures on an individual not to react. Research has consistently shown that the decision whether to intervene is related to the number of people involved, their experience of similar situations, and whether they know the others present. Recent research using the lost letter technique has shown that certain kinds of people are more likely to receive help than others. The research findings have significance for police work, both in enabling officers to understand why people often fail to help, and in making sure that the public becomes more likely to report suspicious incidents.

References

Latané, B. and Darley, J.M. (1970) *The Unresponsive Bystander: Why Doesn't He Help?* New York: Appleton-Century-Crofts.

Further reading

Latané, B. and Darley, J.M. (1970) *The Unresponsive Bystander: Why Doesn't He Help?* New York: Appleton-Century-Crofts.

Rosenthal, A.M. (1964) *Thirty-Eight Witnesses.* New York: McGraw-Hill.
Rushton, J.P. and Sorrentino, R.M. (eds) (1981) *Altruism and Helping Behaviour: Social, Personality and Development Perspectives.* Hillsdale, NJ: Lawrence Erlbaum Associates.
Smithson, M., Amato, P.R. and Pearce P. (1982) *Dimensions of Helping Behaviour.* Oxford: Pergamon.

Chapter 6

People in Groups

In Chapter 5 we showed one way in which behaviour can be affected by the presence of other people. In this chapter we wish to look at some of the other ways in which we may act differently in the presence of others compared with when alone. This is a main interest of that area which we call *social psychology*.

It is a curious fact that although we can see *other* people obviously being influenced by their fellow human beings, we like to imagine our *own* actions as relatively free from the influence of others. We fondly imagine that we make our own independent decisions for our own reasons. A police officer may make a decision whether to arrest a drunk on a Saturday night. There will be many internal factors governing this decision, but the presence of a large group of onlookers will also significantly affect the decision made.

With the rare exception of a hermit or castaway on a desert island we are all social animals. From our arrival in the world we are surrounded by other people, and we gradually learn which behaviour is appropriate in the particular country, region, social class and family in which we find ourselves. Though later on in life we may strive for a certain degree of independence, the process of *socialization* ensures that we learn a whole set of socially appropriate actions. Socialization is a process which does not only occur in childhood. Admission into an occupation like police work will involve a great deal of socialization into that particular sub-culture. You will recognize this sub-culture less and less as you progress in your police service. Essentially it involves the pressure to be seen to be active, brave, resourceful (devious) and straight-speaking. Similarly, the new prison inmate (officer or prisoner) will need to adjust to the many formal and informal rules which operate 'inside'. Even in prison, social life is all important, one of the ultimate punishments being solitary confinement.

Social norms

One of the early psychological experiments on the way our behaviour is affected by others was carried out some 50 years ago by Muzafer Sherif. He had people sit in a completely darkened room. A very small pinpoint of light was visible and the people were asked to indicate when and how far the light moved. In fact the light did not move at all, but most human beings *perceive* its movement in this situation. In the completely darkened room there is no way to measure the distance travelled by the light, so all impressions are subjective. For present purposes, the typical responses of a group of three people in the room together will be examined. In the first session, there is quite wide variation in the perceived distance the light moved. On subsequent occasions, there is less and less variation. Typical results would be as described here:

	1st session	2nd session	3rd session
Person 1	9in	5in	4in
Person 2	3in	4in	3in
Person 3	1in	3in	3in

We can see what is happening here. All three people are modifying their opinion so that it better conforms to that of the other people in the group. In other words, individuals who are faced with an ambiguous task are inclined to look to one another for clues as to the 'correct' answer or the appropriate course of action.

Two other aspects of the Sherif experiment deserve mention. First, when people who had been exposed to the opinions of others in a group were later tested alone, they tended to give replies which the group had decided upon, rather than going back to their original opinion. In other words, the group consensus has an effect which carried over even when the person was no longer with the group. A second important point concerns *awareness* of the influence of other people. When those subjected to this experiment were later interviewed, they largely denied that the other members of the group had affected their responses – despite the evidence of the results. In other words the process of social influence goes largely unnoticed.

Police work and social influence

Let us again relate these findings to police work. Laws, police powers and maximum terms of imprisonment are all laid down by acts of parliament. We know, however, that in practice it would be impossible to enforce every law, or to confine all wrongdoers for the maximum period in prison. Society thus establishes 'social norms' which are an appropriate way of translating law into practice. So, for example, the exercise of police powers owes as much or more to police 'norms' as to the law itself. The sociologist Michael Chatterton described how, in the Division he studied, officers who arrest too many people are looked down on and called 'snatchers' by their colleagues. Those who arrest too few are also looked down on and referred to as 'uniform-carriers'. Community policing similarly operates by establishing norms of behaviour for all members of a community, with the community constable using his or her discretion in a manner appropriate for keeping the peace locally.

An obvious problem arises when the 'norms' of one particular group offend or conflict with the 'norms' (or laws) of another group, resulting in a possible confrontation. Most police forces develop norms which are appropriate for their particular area, in some cases leading to significant differences in policing practices. This was highlighted during the miners' dispute of 1984, when officers from one force were drafted in to work in a different area. Some people complained that officers from an outside force behaved inappropriately. The new constable entering the service will need to adapt to the new norms quickly, and people who do not conform may well be pressured to change their behaviour, or become ostracized from the mainstream of the group. We need not look too far for evidence supporting Sherif's findings!

Group pressure

When published nearly 30 years ago, Sherif's results aroused much interest, especially from other social psychologists, as they offered a neat explanation for the development and sustaining of social norms. However, the question remained as to whether the same results would apply in less ambiguous situations. To test this, Solomon Asch devised an experiment which involved attempting to exert social pressure on an unsuspecting individual in a much less ambiguous situation. A college student entered the laboratory along with seven fellow students. The psychologist explained that the investigation was to test the person's perceptual abilities. Sets of lines of various lengths were shown and compared with a 'standard' line.

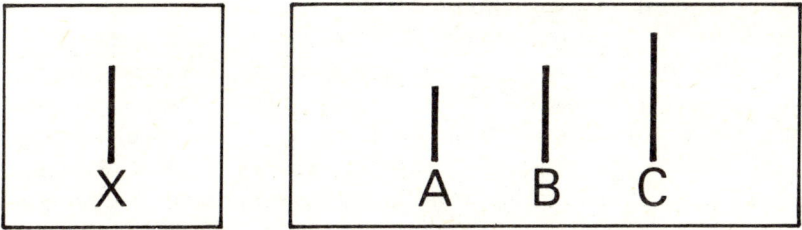

Figure 6.1

In each set, the particular line that equalled the standard line had to be identified. In all, 18 different sets were shown and judged. This seemed a very simple task, and during the first few trials, the person gave the obviously correct answer, and his opinion was confirmed by the identical response of all seven other students. However, on the third trial the person was dismayed to find that all the other people gave a reply which appeared quite obviously wrong. Unknown to the naïve person, the other seven 'students' were confederates of the psychologist and had been instructed to give incorrect answers to 12 of the 18 trials. The naïve person was thus placed in a difficult position. Should he continue to give his own opinion as to the correct reply – or should he bow to the group pressure and give an answer which appeared incorrect?

The results showed that almost three-quarters of those who went through this experimental procedure were unable to resist the group pressure and 'gave in' on at least one occasion. Subsequent research has shown that groups of only three or four are almost as effective in inducing compliance as groups of eight, which was the group size which Asch used. It has also been demonstrated that the pressure of one 'deviant' who goes against the majority will drastically reduce the amount of influence which the rest of the group can exert on someone. In other words, the presence of one ally strengthens the ability to resist the majority, though it may not completely eliminate compliance. Perhaps this fact was known to the legislators who allowed jury decisions to be accepted on a majority of 10 to 2. It seems much less likely that a majority verdict of 11 to 1 would ever occur, because of the intense pressure on the dissenting juror to conform.

What the Asch experiment shows is an example of *conformity*. Behaviour is being altered and controlled by the group. During the experiment, the yielding person learns not to accept his or her own judgement but to use the group's behaviour as a model. In this way, possible ridicule or rejection by the other group members is avoided. The amount of pressure exerted is surprising, given that this was merely a group assembled for the experiment. We suggest that occupational groups or prestigious gangs would be capable of exerting much more pressure than that witnessed here. Although rejection by the particular group in Asch's experiment had no great personal consequences, it seems that most people will have learnt that deviation from group expectations and opinions is often quickly followed by exclusion and a resultant feeling of anxiety. The Asch experiment thus demonstrates in a very effective way just how powerful groups are as agents of social learning, and how much leverage they can exert on the behaviour of any individual member.

Juries

Much work in the field of social psychology involves the study of groups and group processes. For present purposes, we wish to concentrate on one particular type of group – the jury. The jury is one of the cornerstones of the criminal justice system and attacks on the jury are often seen as attempts to undermine the legal system. Social psychological research on groups offers some insights into the workings of the jury. Although the challenging and vetting of members has now become commonplace, especially in North America, an intensive programme at the London School of Economics found that the personality characteristics of jurors and their subsequent verdicts were almost completely uncorrelated. In other words it was not possible to predict whether people would convict or acquit on the basis of knowing their personality. This casts doubt on how often jury challenges alter the verdict in a typical case.

Police officers may often wonder how a jury can have arrived at a particular decision 'despite the evidence'. Social scientists would similarly like to be able to listen to a jury's deliberations, though this particular research technique is not permitted. Nonetheless the influential text *The American Jury* as long ago as 1966 reported a research project which sought to gather some information on jury processes. The procedures in this type of research usually involve interviewing jurors and judges after trials or presenting simulated trials (or transcripts of actual cases) to 'mock juries'. Alternatively, researchers may select a group of twelve people eligible for jury service, sit them in the public gallery, get them to retire somewhere to consider their verdict, and record the whole process. These are known as 'shadow juries'. Perhaps the most frequent technique is the use of mock juries, since this method allows researchers to vary different aspects of the case systematically and test whether this affects the verdict reached. For example, it is possible to study the effect of different victim and defendant characteristics on the outcome. The order of presentation of evidence has also been studied extensively using mock juries. Differences have been found in the eventual decision reached by the jury, according to whether the prosecution or the defence gave evidence first.

This research has demonstrated that a wide variety of extraneous variables may significantly affect jury decisions. Despite the obvious differences between the consequences of the decisions reached by mock and actual juries, the studies give us some pointers to the relevant factors.

An alternative to the use of mock juries is to interview people who have been involved with the case (the police, the judge, solicitors) to assess their opinion of the jury's verdict. This was the procedure used by John Baldwin and Michael McConville in their study *Jury Trials*. Although the prosecution and the defence may well have differing views of the 'correctness' of a verdict, in a significant proportion of over 800 cases studied, the trial judge had serious doubts about the eventual outcome of the jury's decision making. This, you might argue, stems from judicial bias as well as jury bias. However, the researchers found that over 33 per cent of all acquittals and some 5 per cent of convictions were seriously questioned by the trial judge and one other party involved in the case. The researchers found that juries who acquitted tended to stress sympathy or equity, even though the defendant may have been considered 'technically' guilty. For example, the jurors were more likely to return 'Not Guilty' verdicts if the defendant had already suffered or if they knew the sentence was likely to be harsh. Jurors also admitted difficulty in following long complicated cases (such as fraud) and tended to rely on the judge's summing up.

Much of the psychological research on group interaction and decision making helps us to make some sense of jury decisions which appear unusual, or contrary to the evidence in the case. The jury will be ushered into a small room and given little formal guidance on how to reach a decision. For most people it will be a situation of which they have no previous experience. People will be looking for someone to take the initiative to make suggestions as to how to proceed. Anxiety will be lessened considerably if someone announces 'I've been on jury service before, shall I be the foreman?' Other factors besides personal experience and case information may be relevant to understanding interactions within the group of jurors. What about the size, shape, temperature and 'atmosphere' of the jury room? What about the shape of the table? We know of no guidelines on what shape the table should be, and yet psychological research has often demonstrated how social interactions are significantly affected by the shape of the table (see Chapters 2 and 7). The traditional rectangular table will tend to make some people more likely to speak than others, as a simple function of the seat they occupy. For example, the person who sits at the end of the table is three times more likely to be selected as foreman than a person sitting along the side. People who occupy end positions also initiate more communication than those who sit along the sides. Whilst it is undoubtedly true that some members will inevitably be more vocal than others, the rectangular table may well increase the unevenness of participation. If we wish to encourage more even participation in the deliberation and decision making process, then a circular table would make a significant contribution.

It has always been accepted in Britain that a jury is composed of twelve people, and yet we might wish to ask whether this is the best number to have in a group to reach an accurate decision. The question has been much debated in the United States ever since the US Supreme Court was called upon to rule in a case where a defendant appealed against his conviction on the grounds that there were only six people on the jury at his trial (*Williams v. Florida*, 1970). The Supreme Court's basic problem was to establish whether a reduction in the size of the jury adversely affected its functioning. The court decided that the jury's goals were not any less likely to be achieved when the jury numbered only six. This is particularly so where a unanimous decision is required.

However, many psychologists and lawyers who read the Williams decision have now questioned its correctness, largely because the 'evidence' on which it was based was questionable. The Supreme Court made reference to experiments which had little scientific credibility, and in some cases the court completely misunderstood the findings anyway. Eventually the issue was given much more careful consideration in *Ballew v.Georgia*, 1978. Although this was an American case, the decision has much relevance to the United Kingdom. The court in the Ballew case took a great deal of interest in recent social science research and relied on this quite heavily in setting the minimum jury size at six. Psychologists have made reference to the advantages and disadvantages of juries of different sizes.

For example, large juries may well produce a better cross-section of people from the community, but a smaller jury will lead to more even participation by all jury members.

Leaders. We mentioned earlier that the task of a jury is well defined (to reach a verdict) though the method by which this is to be achieved is left to the discretion of the members of the jury. Should they initially take a vote and record their individual opinions immediately? Should they allow a certain length of time for an exchange of views? One way of deciding on the strategy to adopt is for a leader to emerge and to guide the group. A great deal of social psychological research has examined the role of the leader, and indeed who becomes the leader. The role of the 'leader' (in this case the foreman of the jury) may be very important to the eventual outcome. As mentioned earlier, where a person sits at the table greatly influences the probability of selection as foreman. But also relevant is the fact that whoever speaks first is likely to be selected as foreman. Other jury members may well perceive the person who speaks first as the 'obvious' choice as leader and spokesperson, even if his or her opening words were merely asking jury members who should be foreman! It has also been found that males are more likely to be selected as foreman than females, though these findings were made some years ago. We would also suggest that this bias may be partly to do with the sexist title used for the spokesperson of the jury – the foreman!

A further relevant finding is that socio-economic class is associated with selection as foreman. The higher one's socio-economic class (as defined by occupation) the more likely is one's selection as foreman. Therefore, the person most likely to be chosen as foreman is an upper-class male who sits at the end of the table and opens the discussion! These findings are important, as the person elected foreman may have more influence in the group than any other member. Thus the presence of a clearly-defined leader will significantly steer the group's discussions and, perhaps, determine the ultimate decision. Though the leader will tend to be influential, other jurors will make contributions. We should note, however, that participation will inevitably be uneven. Factors relevant to the amount of participation include socio-economic status and level of education. Again, earlier research showed that women contributed less than men, though more recently the difference has declined.

Group polarization. What of the actual discussion that takes place? Psychologists have studied group processes, especially as regards decision shifts. One consistent finding has been that the process of discussion causes some shift in judgement for most group members. This has become known as the 'risky shift' in view of the early finding that individuals are less conservative in their judgements after group discussion than they were before. In fact the so-called 'risky shift' is more accurately referred to as group polarization, the risky shift being an artificial result of the type of problem used in the early studies.

By group polarization we mean that group interaction magnifies already existing tendencies in the individual opinions of members of the group, whatever they are. In other words, if members of a group initially tend to favour one option, then group discussion pushes them further in that direction. Thus if all 12 jury members believe that a defendant is 'more than likely' guilty, then by the end of their discussion, they will be 'absolutely sure' of his guilt. Michael Saks and Reid Hastie express the tendency thus: '... whatever the individual preferences are that enter the deliberation, the final outcome will be an exaggerated version of that distribution of individual judgements.' Whilst this may be seen as a positive sign that jury decisions are an accurate reflection of the opinions of jurors, let us consider the fact that the ultimate decision may be 'an exaggerated version'. Juries in criminal cases are warned that they can only return a guilty verdict if they are satisfied 'beyond all reasonable doubt' that the person is guilty. Whilst acknowledging that the question of what constitutes 'reasonable doubt' is inevitably subjective, group polarization may lead to a higher level of confidence in a guilty verdict than was the case before discussion, or indeed the reaching of a guilty verdict at all.

Group polarization also serves to exert pressure on any minority view to conform to the majority (just as in the Asch experiment, page 66-67). Henry Fonda's accomplishment in changing the opinions of 11 fellow jurors in the film Twelve Angry Men seems an extremely unlikely outcome given research on group processes! Similarly, the number of cases which result in a 'hung' jury are very small. When this does occur it is invariably because group members split into two distinct factions, members receiving social support for their views from their own small 'group'.

Obedience

We have shown how groups exert pressure on individuals to make them conform to certain norms of behaviour, but it is possible for one individual to exert massive control over large numbers of people through demanding obedience. Many of the atrocities of World War II may have originated in the mind of one individual, but even Hitler's wishes could only be carried out if his followers displayed obedience to authority.

In an attempt to gain some understanding of the process of obedience, Stanley Milgram set up an experiment which has become one of the most famous – or infamous – psychological investigations. Milgram wished to establish whether individuals would be prepared to administer considerable pain and suffering to an innocent victim, simply on the command of an experimenter. He informed subjects that they were to take part in an experiment studying the effects of punishment on learning. The 'subjects' were to deliver an electric shock to another person each time he made a mistake on a simple learning task. These shocks were delivered by means of an electric shock generator containing 30 switches. The switches corresponded to various intensity levels from 15 to 450 volts.

The 'learner' was in fact an accomplice of the experimenter who did not actually receive any electric shocks, though subsequent interviews with the subjects confirmed that they believed the shocks were actually delivered. The learner made many errors during the experiment, and each time subjects were expected to deliver an electric shock as punishment for the incorrect answers. They were instructed to increase the shock level with each incorrect answer so that the learner would receive shocks of up to 450 volts if the experiment went through to the end. Subjects soon found themselves in a dilemma. Should they continue to obey the commands of the experimenter and administer severe shocks or simply refuse to carry on? The dilemma was increased when the learner pounded on the wall after the shock level reached 300 volts and from then on refused (or was unable) to answer at all. The subject was told to treat no answer as a wrong answer and to continue increasing the shock levels.

All the subjects were volunteers and had already been paid for merely attending the laboratory. We might therefore predict that very few, if any, would continue to harm the victim simply on the experimenter's instructions. The results were surprising to many commentators: 65 per cent of the subjects showed total obedience and carried on right to the end. We might like to think that if *we* were subjects in this experiment, we would not behave in this apparently sadistic fashion, and yet those who did inflict the maximum shock level were ordinary members of the public, not specially selected psychopaths! The pressures of the situation were such that these people exhibited behaviour which surprised even themselves. The experimental situation generated extreme tension for the subjects. Should they obey the laboratory-coated authority figure of the experimenter? Or should they be concerned with the learner's suffering and stop the experiment? The subjects exhibited many symptoms of this tension – they sweated, trembled and became extremely uncomfortable: yet still some continued to obey.

The results of this initial experiment were disturbing and people drew parallels with wartime atrocities committed against civilians. Other commentators sought to dismiss the results of the experiment as being irrelevant to obedience in the real world. One criticism concerned the fact that the experiment was carried out at Yale University, a high prestige institution, where it might be presumed the 'scientist' knew what he was doing. However, in a further experiment, Milgram obtained similar results when the study was repeated in a rundown office building, with no obvious connection with a 'responsible' institution.

The experimental procedure employed by Milgram was repeated with some variations. For example, in one case the victim was heard to complain loudly of the pain from the shocks and demand to be released – but still over 60 per cent of subjects carried on to the end. A further variation involved having the learner in closer proximity to the subject. In general, the finding was that the further away the learner was, the more obedience occurred. We cannot seek comfort in dismissing the findings as peculiar to the USA, as similar results have been produced as far afield as West Germany and Australia.

Thus the technique adopted by Milgram and others was largely successful in producing high degrees of obedience. There are some aspects of the procedure which no doubt contributed to the results, and we now consider some of these.

First, the experimenter was dressed in a laboratory coat and was referred to as 'Doctor ...' This would undoubtedly serve to confer a high degree of status on the experimenter, who would be looked up to. Similarly, although the naïve subjects actually pressed the switch to deliver the shock, the ultimate responsibility could be shifted onto the experimenter – 'I was just obeying orders'.

A further point concerns the way in which the shock levels were *gradually* increased from the initial very mild 15 volts to the eventual 450 volts. At the beginning of the experiment subjects did not know how many mistakes the learner would make. They may have presumed that the experiment might only involve administering a few mild shocks. There is a well-established principle in psychology which in everyday language is referred to as the 'foot in the door technique'. This refers to the fact that if you wish people to oblige a large request, their cooperation is more likely if you initially make a small request. You may have noticed door-to-door salespersons using a variant of this technique. If the first question was 'Would you like to spend £2,000 on double glazing from my company?' it is unlikely you would immediately say 'Yes'. However, if the first question is as innocent as 'Would you mind answering a few questions?' you are much more likely to be cooperative. Having gained your cooperation in this way, the skilled seller will *gradually* increase the level of demands made until the final agreement to buy is signed.

The effectiveness of the technique has been demonstrated in psychological experiments as well as in the sales figures of double glazing companies! One of the best-known experiments involved a number of householders being contacted by telephone and asked a few simple questions about the type of soap they used at home. A few days later, the same people were approached with a much larger request. They were asked if they would agree to allow a team of five people into their home for two hours in order to make an inventory of all products in the house. The householders were asked to grant complete freedom to the five men to search thoroughly all drawers, cabinets, etc. The researchers found that over half the people who had consented to the earlier, simple request now agreed to this major invasion of their home. As a comparison, less than a quarter of a further sample of householders who were approached directly with the large request agreed to let the men into the house.

Many other studies have confirmed the effectiveness of this technique in eliciting compliance. For example, it has been demonstrated to be effective in persuading people to sign a petition, to contribute to charity and, in another experiment, to allow the erection of a massive hoarding in someone's front garden! The explanation for the success of the foot in the door technique rests with the fact that human beings like to appear consistent in their behaviour. Agreeing to a small unobtrusive request leads to a subtle change in people's self-image – they may begin to see themselves as the sort of person who is helpful. In order to maintain this self-image, people agree to larger requests and the behaviour is seen as consistent with the initial act of helping. Agreeing to a small request may also serve to persuade the individual that these 'helping' situations are not as unpleasant as they might have imagined. The skilled interrogator may well use the foot in the door technique. By answering simple, trivial questions, the person will start to comply with the interrogator's requests for information. The interviewing officers can then build up the questions so that the suspect continues to answer more serious, probing questions.

Let us return to the Milgram experiment for a moment. You will recall that subjects had to increase the level of shock by 15 volts each time: there were 30 switches to be pressed before the final 450 volts' level was reached. Subjects who agreed to obey the relatively less serious command to administer 15 volts would be likely to continue the gradual increase in order to remain consistent in their behaviour. The amount of obedience to the command to deliver large voltage shocks may have been significantly reduced if earlier, less demanding requests had not been made. Similarly, if Milgram had provided a convenient 'break off' point by *suddenly* increasing the voltage level, this may well have led more people to stop obeying at that point. It is interesting to note that the point where the first subject disobeyed the experimenter's commands was when the victim pounded on the wall. The 'disobedient' subjects presumably saw this as a significant change and a new dimension to the experiment – a convenient 'break off' point.

The disturbing results, and the methods, of the Milgram experiments have been a talking point for many years. A number of people have questioned the ethics of experiments of this kind, though Milgram suggests it is the results which are disturbing rather than the experimental procedure. In this, as in the Asch experiment, subjects were deceived as to the true purpose of the experiment, and the practice is quite common in social psychology experiments. The reason is that people alter their behaviour if they are aware of what the experiment is investigating. Further, how people *think* they will behave is often very different from how they *actually* behave. Very few people (including the subjects themselves) could have predicted the high level of obedience which was ultimately found. Debates continue as to the nature of obedience in the outside world. Parallels can be drawn between the Milgram situation and everyday events, and this study has added something to our understanding of obedience. Armies train the lower ranks to be obedient. Street corner gangs demand conformity and obedience. The police service would also find it difficult to function without some degree of obedience to authority though, as many sociologists have pointed out, even direct orders are often translated or modified by the officers working the streets. While obedience is a necessary part of most societies, unquestioning obedience has been seen as a major factor in many atrocities carried out during wartime. A number of the people who took part in Milgram's experiments later reported that they were glad to have done so as it taught them something about themselves which they would not have believed. Learning about their behaviour may also give you some insights into the pressures to which we may all succumb.

Police officers are no doubt only too well aware that the behaviour of any one individual will be considerably altered by the presence of a large crowd. The football crowd, the large demonstration, the mass picket and mass policing will all tend to lead individuals to perform acts which they would hardly ever consider if they were alone. The presence of large numbers of people often seems to weaken restraints against engaging in impulsive or antisocial behaviour. This tendency is referred to as *deindividuation*. It is a common enough occurrence, and an explanation of the phenomenon would seem appropriate at this stage. Though we may have certain views on the type of person who goes to football matches, the fact remains that most people taking part in acts of mass vandalism or even riots may never consider committing these antisocial acts when alone. Indeed individuals are often amazed at their own behaviour when the crowd has dispersed and they are left alone to consider their actions.

So how are we to make sense of the process of deindividuation? Psychologists have suggested an explanation in terms of private self-awareness. We maintain our personal and social standards of behaviour by tuning into or being aware of our own feelings, behaviour and opinions. Deindividuation occurs when this self-awareness is interrupted by certain environmental conditions. These conditions include anonymity, a high level of arousal, close group unity and a focus on *external* events and goals. Under these conditions, self-awareness is sharply reduced and the individual's whole perception and experience is altered. Consequently the indiviual will find it more difficult to monitor or regulate his or her actions. The deindividuated state will also mean that the individual is less likely to think *rationally* or to consider long-term consequences. It will also reduce the usual concern over how others will evaluate his or her behaviour.

As an example of deindividuation, let us take the case of the policing of a major public disorder. This situation allows:

- *anonymity* – due to the high numbers of similar uniforms

- *high arousal* – particularly if the situation is violent, when fear and increased adrenalin would result in heightened arousal

- *group unity* – members of police support units often travel together and see themselves as a cohesive group and foster a group image.

Deindividuation occurs in many different situations and may produce behaviour ranging from the unusual or annoying to the violent and destructive. But do such explanations or theories have any practical value? Robert Baron and Donn Byrne suggest that through our understanding of the process of deindividuation it is possible to suggest techniques for countering some of its effects. They suggest, for example, that we should aim to counter the feeling of anonymity by making individuals believe they can be identified singularly. Though police officers will rarely be able to identify single faces in a crowd, photographs or videotapes may make the individual feel vulnerable to later identification. Perhaps this is one of the reasons for so much publicity being given to the introduction of Hooli-vans at soccer matches.

A second strategy suggested by Baron and Byrne would be to enhance self-awareness. We showed earlier how members of a large crowd shift their attention outwards and temporarily forget their own values or attitudes. If we can prevent this shift of focus, then the individual is more likely to be constrained in his or her behaviour. In this respect, we might consider enhancing self-awareness through showing people an image of themselves through closed circuit TV or special reflectors.

These are, of course, only tentative suggestions made with the limited knowledge gained from research in this area. It is argued that deindividuation, like most other bases of behaviour, can be controlled once the processes of its operation are understood. Given the realities of crowd behaviour witnessed nearly every day, this research represents an area of great importance for psychologists and police officers alike.

Review notes

Although we may like to think of ourselves as fairly independent and able to resist pressure from other people, research in social psychology has repeatedly demonstrated just how easily we can be influenced by others. Early experiments by Solomon Asch and Muzafer Sherif showed how group pressures can affect our judgements, even though we may be unaware of this effect. Social psychological research on groups may help us to understand some of the stranger decisions which juries return. For example, the shape of the table, the choice of foreman and the size of the jury may all have a significant effect on decision making.

Obedience may be a necessary part of everyday life and a series of experiments by Stanley Milgram demonstrated just how obedient people can be, given appropriate circumstances.

The presence of a large number of other people may well lead individuals to perform acts which they would not consider when alone. The phenomenon of *deindividuation* can explain some of the behaviour of individuals when in a crowd.

References

Baldwin, J. and McConville, M. (1979) *Jury Trials*. Oxford: Clarendon Press.
Baron, R.A. and Byrne, D. (1984) *Social Psychology: Understanding Human Interaction*, 4th ed. Boston: Allyn & Bacon.
Kalven, H. and Zeisel, H. (1966) *The American Jury*. Boston: Little and Brown.
Milgram, S. (1974) *Obedience to Authority*. New York: Harper.
Saks, M.J. and Hastie, R. (1978) *Social Psychology in Court*. New York: Van Nostrand Reinhold.
Sealy, A. and Cornish, W. (1973) Jurors and their verdicts. *Modern Law Review, 36*, 496–508.

Further reading

Baron, R.A. and Byrne, D. (1984) *Social Psychology: Understanding Human Interaction*, 4th ed. Boston: Allyn & Bacon.
Devons, E. (1964) Serving as a juryman in Britain. *Modern Law Review, 28*, 561–570.
Konecni, V.J. and Ebbesen, E.B. (1982) *The Criminal Justice System: A Social Psychological Analysis*. San Francisco: Freeman.
Saks, M.J. and Hastie, R. (1978) *Social Psychology in Court*. New York: Van Nostrand Reinhold.

Chapter 7

Places and Crimes

Whenever we observe people behaving in a certain way we tend to make inferences about *why* they are behaving that way. Often we will assume they behave badly because of something within their basic personality. They are just bad people. Sometimes we accept that their experience in life has made them behave like that, and that if we had gone through the same experience we would behave like that too. Psychologists have long since recognized that it is not helpful to think in this either/or sort of way. Any piece of behaviour is caused by an *interaction* between a person's nature and the environment in which the behaviour takes place. Different environments will have different effects on people according to their personalities – one man's meat ... Psychologists no longer talk about the extent to which behaviour is caused by nature or environment, but rather about the interaction between the two, and the relative contribution of each. Sometimes even thinking in terms of relative contributions is nonsense. What is the relative contribution to the flavour of a cake of its ingredients (nature) and cooking (environment)?

Apart from the general tendency to think of human behaviour as the result of *either* heredity *or* environment, there is a closely related mistake which people make and which is fundamental. Let us introduce the fundamental attribution error. No, do not close the book. It is not just jargon, and we will explain it. The fundamental attribution error is the name given to the fact that people typically *underestimate* the situation as cause of behaviour and *overestimate* an individual's nature as the cause of behaviour. For example, even when a piece of behaviour occurs under irresistible duress, there is some change in how the person under duress is viewed. You have only to think of those war films where someone has broken down and talked under torture. Try as you might, you cannot help thinking of the victim as less brave, even if the torture was extreme. This tendency to see the person rather than the situation as causing events is a general one, and we should not have to spell out its important implications for how, for instance, rape victims are viewed.

A particularly neat demonstration of the error comes in the work of psychologists who set up a general knowledge quiz game. Randomly, one person was assigned the role of questioner, another the role of contestant, a third the role of observer. The questioner had to make up a set of difficult general knowledge questions, ask the contestant these questions and then give the right answer where the contestant had got it wrong. Later, questioner, contestant and observer were asked to rate the questioner's and the contestant's general knowledge. Both contestant and observer in this situation consistently rated the questioner as superior to the contestant in general knowledge. Clearly this is an unjustified conclusion, because the set-up allows the contestant chances to show ignorance which are denied to the questioner, and allows the questioner opportunities to demonstrate knowledge which are denied to the contestant. Despite this, the observers make the fundamental attribution error. Things which should really be put down to differences between the situations in which people were placed were instead put down to differences between people themselves.

Given the fundamental attribution error, psychologists have a responsibility to show the ways in which the environment affects behaviour, and over the last 20 years they have turned more and more to this task. Chapters 5 and 6 deal with the extent to which the social environment affects behaviour, and this is also touched on in Chapter 13, as it affects crime victims. Here we show some of the ways in which the physical environment may influence behaviour and apply this to the topic of crime prevention.

Prison life

In Chapter 6 we showed how a number of normal people could be made to administer what they thought were lethal electric shocks to a victim simply because they were told to do so by an authority figure. There is no doubt that certain features of that situation contributed to the large amount of obedience observed. For example, the fact that the victim was in another room and the authority figure was in the same room is relevant. You may know of the mandarin problem, beloved of moral philosophers, where you are asked if you would press a button to kill a Chinese person thousands of miles away, with the guarantee that you would never be caught and would inherit his fortune. The value of the problem here is that it illustrates the fact that if the death you cause is far enough away, you are tempted to get away with murder.

Perhaps an even more dramatic illustration of the power of social pressure is provided by a much reported study which examined behaviour in a simulated prison. Just think for a moment about your preconceptions of prison officers and prisoners. We may be inclined to think that people decide to become prison officers because of something in their basic personalities. Perhaps this is true. The important point is that if you believe that prison officers chose their job because of their basic personality, their subsequent behaviour in that job would be assumed to be largely a function of the type of people they are. Similarly, prisoners are in prison because they have done wrong. Their wrongdoing and their behaviour in prison would be assumed to be the product of some personality defect.

However, an experiment by Phillip Zimbardo and his colleagues in the USA showed that the behaviour of both guards and prisoners may well be largely determined by the prison environment itself. Zimbardo had a number of people come forward to volunteer for his study. He selected 24 mature, emotionally stable college students from middle-class homes. By the flip of a coin, half of the volunteers were designated guards and half prisoners. The 'guards' were allowed to make up their own rules for maintaining order in the simulated prison and to revise the rules as the experiment went on. The 'prisoners' were given a uniform and expected to live three to a cell. They were paid a significant amount of money to act as prisoners, and they had volunteered. The experiment was scheduled to run for two weeks but had to be stopped after only six days because of what happened. Although all the subjects were undoubtedly playing a role at the start of the experiment, after a few days both guards and prisoners seemed unclear about where reality ended and their role began.

Phillip Zimbardo (1972) reported:

There were dramatic changes in virtually every aspect of their behaviour, thinking and feeling. In less than a week the experience of imprisonment ended (temporarily) a lifetime of learning; human values were suspended, self-concepts were challenged and the ugliest, most base, psychological side of human nature surfaced. We were horrified because we saw some boys (guards) treat others as if they were despicable animals, taking pleasure in cruelty, while other boys (prisoners) became servile, dehumanised robots who thought only of escape, of their own individual survival and of their mounting hatred for the guards.

This example serves to demonstrate just how powerful can be the influence of an environment. It may be dangerous for us to be complacent and claim that *we* would never behave in such a way. As Zimbardo points out, we all tend to create an illusion of freedom by assuming that *we* have more internal control of our behaviour than is the case. By doing this, we fall into the trap of the fundamental attribution error.

City life

All our behaviour takes place within some kind of physical setting and most of these settings are likely to be more or less 'man-made'. A significant proportion of the world's population now lives in large cities, although the urban migration has been quite sudden and quite recent. In 1850 only 2 per cent of the world's population lived in cities of more than 100,000 people. The figure is now about 25 per cent and it is estimated that by the end of the century some 40 per cent of the world's population will be living in cities of this size. People have thus had to adapt rapidly from their previous mode of existence to life in the more complex and fast-moving environment of the city.

Many writers have talked of cities being 'human jungles' where behaviour becomes pathological in a number of ways. In fact, much of the so-called evidence is based on subjective impressions rather than hard data. There is without doubt a higher rate of crime and mental illness in cities. The difficult question is why? There are many factors which go to make cities as they are. Migration of people into cities is not random. Loss of land is a major reason for immigration to city ghettos in many countries. The search for work is a significant reason for many British people heading towards London.

Cities are often overcrowded. They provide more crime opportunities. The diversity of city activities is staggering compared with what would be possible in a rural environment. However, the city is also a more complex environment and requires swift and frequent decisions to be made. Walking down a busy city centre street we may be bombarded with information or demands from other people. Stanley Milgram argued that the city has so much going on that we are constantly in danger of being overloaded with information. He noted that people can only absorb so much information at any one time, and that in order to avoid information overload, we develop adaptive responses such as:

- Allocating less time to each input.
- Disregarding what are considered to be 'low priority' inputs (like the newspaper seller or the street cleaner).
- Discouraging or blocking off unwanted intrusions (by leaving the phone off the hook or wearing a frown or a scowl).
- Diminishing the intensity of inputs so that only weak and superficial forms of involvement need ensue.

Milgram suggests that the ultimate adaptation to an overloaded environment involves disregarding the needs and demands of all those others who one feels are not relevant to one's personal needs. Psychologists have demonstrated that people who live in cities are likely to be less helpful than people who live in a rural setting, though some have suggested that this difference is due to the greater fear of crime in cities. Undoubtedly some aspects of cities make them more attractive to the criminal (greater opportunity, more anonymity, greater networks for fencing stolen goods), and this is discussed later.

One feature of modern city life which has received considerable attention from psychologists is noise and its effects on human behaviour. Noise can be a considerable source of stress, as many a complaint call made to the police will testify. Excessive noise may not only make us feel uncomfortable, but may also affect our physical wellbeing and our ability to learn. People tend to be less helpful in a noisy environment than in a quiet one.

Crowds and behaviour

Anxiety over the consequences of living in overcrowded conditions has stemmed largely from research carried out with animals. John Christian, for example, noted that some animal populations suffered a sudden crash in numbers when density reached a certain level. Post-mortem examinations tended to suggest that the animals had been severely stressed in high density conditions, and the high stress had led to increased rates of mortality. More systematic studies using rats and mice were carried out by Robert Calhoun. In one experiment Calhoun put a small number of mice into a protected environment. The mice were given as much food and water as they needed and were shielded from any outside threat. Calhoun studied how the population developed, and expected that within a few weeks it would increase dramatically.

The living quarters of the mice were divided into four compartments. Some of the compartments were linked whilst others were not. Calhoun observed the mice and found that some of the worst conduct occurred in the pens which were the most crowded. He described how the whole social order disintegrated in the most crowded pens, which he described as a 'behavioural sink'. He noted how many of the new mouse pups (up to 96 per cent) would die during the first few days of life, thus limiting population increase. He described how some of the females became completely abnormal (for mice), fulfilling no sexual or maternal functions and merely huddling with the male mice. The male mice could actually be divided into four 'social classes':

- dominant males who behaved relatively normally
- pansexuals who did not discriminate among sexual partners
- somnambulists who completely withdrew themselves
- probers who were hyperactive, hypersexual and cannibalistic.

Various psychologists have questioned whether these experiments suggest a mouse-like end to the human race! Ormer Galle took a number of measures of human pathology (mortality ratio, fertility rate, percentage of families on public assistance, rate of recorded juvenile delinquency and the rate of admissions to mental hospitals) and found that they were associated statistically with overcrowding. Four of the five measures showed increases when appropriate measures of density were used (that is, the number of persons per room). One psychologist has shown that in prisons (typically an example of high density living) inmates are more likely to fall ill or to commit suicide as population size increases. Others have even suggested that overcrowded prisons may be those which produce higher rates of recidivism. In a study of cities in the USA, another psychologist has shown that the number of recorded rapes, robberies, murders and car thefts increases as the size of the community increases.

Insofar as density is a cause, it may not be high density *as such* that has the effect, but rather whether the high density gives rise to a feeling of overcrowding. Galle's research showed that the number of people per acre was not associated with pathology, but the number of people per room was. It also seems to be the case that human beings can show (up to a point) adaptations to high density living (think of Tokyo or Hong Kong). Living in conditions *experienced* as overcrowded is undoubtedly stressful as it denies us our proper share of personal space and privacy.

A further aspect of the environment which psychologists have studied is heat and its possible effect on aggression. Early studies showed that there was a relationship in that as the temperature rose so did the amount of aggression shown by individuals. This was offered as one explanation for why riots only seem to occur during the summer months. However, some later research tended to question this and showed an opposite effect (that is, a rise in temperature led to less aggression). It has now been established that heat does have an effect on aggression but the relationship is not a straightforward one. Increases in temperature do lead to increases in aggression, but only up to a certain point. When the temperature rises beyond the critical level, further increases serve to *reduce* the amount of aggression displayed. So the summers when large scale disturbances are likely are warmish rather than very hot. This fits in, surely, with personal experience. There comes a point at which you just want to lie down and sweat.

Architectural environment

In Chapter 2 we showed some of the ways in which the layout of rooms and furniture can affect behaviour. It is also true that behaviour will be affected by the design of housing and offices. When slum clearance programmes were announced in the 1950s and 60s it was expected by many that moving people into more modern housing would, along with other social reforms of the time, cure a great many social problems. Unfortunately, many of the so-called solutions created more problems than they solved. In Britain and America, many tower blocks and deck access flats have had to be demolished before the end of their design life, in some cases even before the local authority had paid for their construction.

It is easy to be critical with hindsight. Most architects did not foresee the problems created by moving families into tower blocks. William Yancey (1971) has written of how a new housing project in St Louis Missouri became a nightmare for the families who lived there and the buildings had to be demolished within a few years of their erection. Yancey argued that the project failed largely because the physical design did not allow development of informal social networks which had been a feature of life for the working-class families in their previous homes.

No doubt you can think of an area in a town or city where there are many problems and widespread fear of crime, where people want to move out as fast as possible and where it is difficult to discern any form of social life. This is the kind of area where the slogan 'Watch out, there's a neighbour about' is likely to replace the original version. It's easier to recognize areas like this than to know what to do about them.

Environmental psychology has a link with criminology. In the frontier area between the two, until recently the most popular approach to the question of how to plan places freer from crime was derived from the 'defensible space' theory, developed by Oscar Newman. Newman was Director of the Institute of Planning and Housing at New York University. He identified a particular type of building as crime prone. It was high-rise with long dark corridors, lifts and easy access to people with no right to be there. Four characteristics of good design were identified by Newman as being likely to reduce crime through the encouragement of a sense of ownership and community. These were:

Territoriality: buildings and grounds should be subdivided into 'zones of influence', so that any part of a building or its surroundings should 'belong' to one dwelling unit's zone of influence. It does not have to be actual ownership, just obvious oversight. You may recall the research on bystander apathy described in Chapter 5. That research showed that one reason for not helping was an apparent diffusion of responsibility. When it was not obvious who was responsible for helping, people tended not to help. In the same way, unzoned grounds or stairwells, for example, *diffuse* responsibility for action.

Surveillance: buildings must be designed to allow easy observation of territorial 'zones'. There is not much point in zoning areas (by paths, hedges, colour schemes, etc.) if you can not actually *see* your bit of territory.

Image: the design of public housing to avoid the stigma of inferiority. Here, you might feel, Newman has made an important point. Having felt it, you are unlikely to disagree with him about the need to avoid the depressing, badly insulated and tatty public housing which we are all able to identify from our own experience.

Environment: mixing up public and safe private housing developments. The ultimate in this mixing process comes with the sale of many council houses. It is a safe bet that estates where many houses have been sold have less crime and more community spirit than estates without sales. But it is *not* necessarily that way because Newman was right. It is a safe bet because housing estates with a better spirit and less fear happen also to be the ones where people want to buy their homes.

Newman's work is unusual in social science. He actually told people what to do to prevent crime. Unfortunately, when they went out to put Newman's ideas into practice, they did not always work. Sheena Wilson (1980) looked at vandalism in some 285 housing blocks of a variety of designs in 38 council estates in inner London. She showed that child density, rather than design factors, was the most important factor in determining level of vandalism. However, when child densities were below an apparently 'critical' level, defensible space features did seem to reduce vandalism. Other research also showed that while social factors like child density and social composition of residents were critical, design features were also important in the way Newman suggested. The level of caretaking and maintenance was also crucial. Very recently, design features have again been stressed as important, and the forthcoming work of Alice Coleman of King's College, London will no doubt be well publicized.

So what?

What does all this amount to? We think it shows that design features are important, but you have got to tackle problem estates across a broad front. Sheena Wilson's research illustrates this. She showed that design features come into play when child densities were not very high. Swamp the place with children and design effects disappear. That must mean that local authority architects' departments and housing departments are both relevant to a solution. Average child density *and* appropriate design features will, put together, have an effect. This is easier to say than to achieve, but then anything worthwhile is. Getting local authority departments to *collaborate* is difficult. The fact that it is now Home Office policy to encourage such collaboration (by Home Office Circular 8/84) is not thought likely to make a dramatic improvement.

One way to foster community spirit in public housing estates is through mobilizing resident effort. NACRO (the National Association for the Care and Resettlement of Offenders and the Prevention of Crime) has established many such projects. These typically take the pattern:

● Detailed consultation with the residents, leading to a set of recommendations for action.

- Negotiations with the agencies involved, particularly the local authority, over implementation.
- Monitoring the effects.

A similar general strategy is employed in the Department of the Environment's Priority Estates project. The involvement of the residents in this way is likely to be good on psychological grounds if only because it removes the sense of helplessness (see Chapter 13). However, as relations between police and residents improve, and as residents begin to feel that something *can* be done about crime in their area, they may begin to report more crime and make it appear that crime increased or held steady. This is always a problem in interpreting crime rates. There will certainly be a time in your career when an increase in recorded crime rates indicates success. The psychology behind the decision to report a crime to the police is crucial.

As was hinted earlier, implementation of sound proposals for change is perhaps the biggest problem. It is here that police officers can play a useful role. An example of the problem might help. A Home Office project to reduce vandalism in schools foundered for the following reasons, among others:

- The replacement of vulnerable windows with damage-resistant glazing never happened, even though it had been agreed, because the large number of different sized panes meant that it would have been difficult to store a few standard sized panes in readiness, and the suppliers who had been approached estimated that it would take up to six weeks to supply and fit a pane of toughened glass. It was thought that this would be unacceptable.

- The relocation of a playing area had been sub-contracted but in the process a misunderstanding arose which led to only half the proposed area having been resurfaced *two years* later.

- The school which was most hit by vandalism employed a force of education department caretakers to patrol the school for overtime payment, outside school hours. However, other schools and other caretakers demanded a similar facility. The cost rose as coverage was extended to other schools. Ultimately the cost became too high and the scheme was scrapped.

If something like this could happen to a showpiece Home Office project, it beggars the imagination to think of what might happen to run-of-the-mill local initiatives. We tell this tragi-comic story because it shows that the recognition of the importance of environmental factors is only the first step of a long journey. Chapter 11 describes the psychological study of the criminal, concluding that an emphasis on how to deal with the criminal does not have too much to do with what can be done about crime.

Since crime prevention is the *first* priority in the Act establishing a police force in this country, it is right to be aware of what can be done by modifying people's environment and what difficulties are presented. Every time a member of the public describes a crime problem in passing to a member of the police force, the response can either set up a chain of events towards crime prevention or just stop there. To take an example from one of the priority estates in the project mentioned earlier, the arrangements for emptying a skip filled with rubble from building renovation was an important link in preventing nuisance offences involving the contents of the skip.

Another way in which consciousness of environmental effects can be put to good use is through community initiatives on crime prevention. Virtually every such initiative spawns a committee and virtually every such committee has a police representative. Often the rank of the officer represents the opinion the force holds of the initiative. Certainly, whatever the rank of the police representative, their attitude to environment change has been far from consistently helpful. Perhaps the idea that bad people do bad things is too ingrained.

But is the environment out there?

Some police officers will argue that it is the police force which has been consistent in accepting the effects of the environment on behaviour, and criminologists, including psychologists of crime, are just jumping on the bandwagon. It is true that police crime prevention officers have long emphasized target hardening to prevent crime. It is true that crime prevention is steadily (albeit unevenly) increasing in the priority it attracts within the police service, and that crime prevention advice will be expected more and more from all officers, not just those specially trained. However two other things are also true.

- With some notable exceptions, the highest calibre of officer is not attracted to crime prevention, and much local crime prevention practice is unimaginative and probably largely ineffective.

- Environments exist in the mind. By this we mean that you have to take into account how other people see the same place.

A very good example of this comes in attempts to prevent burglary. Standard police crime prevention advice stresses adequate door and window locks in adequate frames. This advice assumes that items of security hardware are key aspects of the environment. Seeing the hardware, the assumption goes, the potential burglar is deterred. *All* the research which actually asks burglars how they choose their targets shows that this view is wrong, and that hardware is not seen as a major obstacle by most burglars. What burglars primarily avoid are houses with signs of occupancy. In other words, the environment which the unimaginative crime prevention officer assumes the burglar is seeing is quite different from the environment which the burglar actually inhabits. This sort of mismatch completely vitiates the value of opportunity reduction approaches. Neighbourhood Watch Schemes, insofar as they are successful, work because the potential burglar's *perception* of the situation is subtly changed. It is highly unlikely that a neighbour will actually be looking around the net curtains as the potential burglar walks past. It is how the burglar *sees* the situation that is crucial. The same is true also, in a very different way, for property marking.

Particularly in the area of crime prevention, there is scope for the imaginative police officer to think in ways which may reduce crime and disorder by modification of settings, rather than people. This may take some lateral thinking, and may well lead away from the normal mainstream of police activity. The former head of the Home Office Crime Prevention Centre at Stafford tells a story of how late night taking of motor cars from a city centre was reduced by rearrangement of bus schedules. Making crash helmets compulsory reduces the incidence of theft of motor cycles (think about the scope for opportunistic theft there). Neighbourhood Watch, property marking and priority estate schemes provide a fertile ground for the officer wishing to use and develop an understanding of the environment's role in discouraging criminal behaviour.

It should be clear that environmental psychology must be taken into account in addressing crime problems. A police officer who tries to prevent crime without taking the psychology of places into account is almost certain to fail. There is a great deal of stale, tired 'locks, bolts and bars' crime prevention which is nothing more than a knee-jerk reflex to crime problems. It could be done better.

Review notes

Environments put heavy pressure on people to behave in particular ways. Research has shown that prison life and city life are strange ways of life to which people adapt, sometimes in ways which make us see them as cruel and uncaring. In cities, people tend to 'cut themselves off' in public places, feel stressed by the sense of overcrowding, and respond to moderately high temperatures with aggression.

Architecture also changes behaviour. The theory of defensible space suggests ways in which buildings could be designed to reduce rates of crime, but social factors like child density are also important. Collaboration in the design and implementation of crime prevention initiatives should include an enthusiastic police contribution from an officer with working knowledge of the relevant environmental psychology.

The perception of crime opportunities is a crucial aspect of design, since people may differ in the ways in which they see the potential of situations for crime.

References

Calhoun, J.B. (1962) Population density and social pathology. *Scientific American*, *206*, 139–148.
Galle, O.R., Gove, W.R. and McPherson, J.M. (1972) Population density and pathology: what are the relations for man? *Science, 176*, 23–30.
Milgram, S. (1970) The experience of living in cities. *Science, 167*, 1461–1468.
Newman, O. (1973) *Defensible Space*. New York: Macmillan.
Wilson, S. (1980) Vandalism and defensible space on London housing estates. In R.V.G. Clarke (ed.) *Tackling Vandalism*. (Home Office Research Study 37.) London: HMSO.
Zimbardo, P.G. (1972) Pathology of imprisonment. *Society, 9*, No. 6.

Further reading

Brantingham, P. and Brantingham, P. (eds) (1981) *Environmental Criminology*. Beverly Hills: Sage.
Moos, R.H. (1976) *The Human Context: Environmental Determinants of Behavior*. New York: Wiley.

Chapter 8

Prejudice and Discrimination

The topics of prejudice and discrimination are generally emotionally highly charged. The allegation of racial prejudice and discrimination in particular is likely to be emotive. This is especially likely to arouse passions among police officers and among members of ethnic communities. Race riots have occurred from time to time. The 1981 British riots, in Brixton, Toxteth and elsewhere, although not strictly race riots at all, marked a significant change in official attitudes, particularly since Lord Scarman's report identified police tactics as being a contributory factor in the flashpoint of the Brixton disturbances. The riots have also led the Home Office to place relations between police and ethnic communities much closer to the centre of the policy stage. This is obvious in its 1984 statement of criminal justice policy. In that document, the Home Office is clearly preoccupied. Nearly every time the word 'community' is used, the real meaning is obviously 'ethnic minority community'. The 1983 report of the Policy Studies Institute on the Metropolitan Police made public a great deal of racist talk by the police, and some evidence of clumsiness or worse in dealing with ethnic minorities. It was no longer possible for the police service to hide behind denials of a problem (although there are still huge differences of opinion on what the precise problem is). The establishment of a centre for relevant training and research at Brunel University also signalled Home Office concern.

A variety of national and local policies and initiatives have taken place during the last few years. In short, we know and you know that this is a live problem. In circumstances like this, people take up positions, and tend not to listen when new information is presented. They are also inclined to see criticism where none is intended (as well as where it is intended!). We have therefore divided this chapter into two parts.

The first deals with what psychologists know about prejudice and discrimination. In this part of the chapter we provide a background of research and basic theory, distanced a little from the sensitive real-life issues to which they are relevant. In the second part of the chapter we apply the lessons of the first part to the difficult and confused real world. In this way, we have tried to separate what we know about prejudice and discrimination from what we should *do* about it. What we should do must always be a matter of judgement, not just a matter of fact.

We regard the alienation of the police service from ethnic communities as an exceptionally dangerous development. We have in mind something that has already been a feature of life in Northern Ireland, namely the alienation of the Royal Ulster Constabulary from nationalist communities, with the development of a 'shadow' criminal justice (?) system operated by paramilitary forces, paralleling the official system. The situation is not beyond hope in Great Britain, but we feel that forceful actions are necessary and we have written forcefully about them in the second part of this chapter. We also regard discrimination by gender as an important issue. More generally, we see recruitment, training, evaluation and promotion in the police service as areas in which discrimination (not necessarily racial or sexual) can be practised.

Distinguishing prejudice and discrimination

In principle, there is a simple distinction between prejudice and discrimination. Prejudice involves holding a particular *attitude* towards a social group, and discrimination is *acting on the basis of* your prejudice. Prejudice can be favourable or unfavourable. You can be prejudiced in favour of a group as much as you can be prejudiced against it. Sometimes the two are just opposite sides of the same coin. Being prejudiced against black or brown people is effectively the same as being prejudiced in favour of white people. Being prejudiced against women is the same as being prejudiced in favour of men. Although prejudice can be either favourable or unfavourable, the term is almost always used to indicate unfavourable attitudes.

In some definitions of prejudice, there is the idea of prejudice as an attitude based on inadequate information (that is, pre-judging). Clearly if you are prepared to judge people only by the colour of their skin or their sex, you are prejudiced. In a current advertising campaign on behalf of disabled people, the slogan reads 'They only see the (wheel)chair, not the person'. The problem comes when you ask questions like 'Can you be prejudiced against members of the National Front?' If prejudice involves an attitude towards a social group based on inadequate information, you have to ask yourself whether knowing someone is a National Front member is or is not enough to make a judgement about them. The concept of prejudice is fuzzy because it is based on a judgement of the information which is thought adequate to make a judgement. To some extent, the identification of prejudice is based on God-like detachment from the real world. Otherwise, who is to say when you know enough to make a judgement?

Despite the fuzziness, it should be clear to all fair-minded people that judgements based purely on skin colour or sex or religion alone must be regarded as prejudiced. You simply cannot make reliable judgements about people from these characteristics. Since it is prejudice against people on these lines which presents us with the really acute social problems, we do not have to be too obsessed about definitions.

Discrimination is prejudice in action. Although in its obvious forms it involves action (assaults on Asians, stop and search without good reason, booing and throwing bananas at black footballers), it can be much more subtle, like failing to intervene in disputes because of the skin colour of the disputants, not reacting promptly to requests for help, driving your bus past request stops after seeing the skin colour of those waiting to board, and so on. In a sense, if you are prejudiced, it is difficult to see how you can avoid being discriminatory even in such trivial things as whether and how to start up a conversation. Many of the examples in Chapter 3 are also relevant here. Perception, it was there stressed, is always an interpretation of sense data. Weapons are shifted in perception from the hand of a white person to the hand of a black person. You see in part what you expect to see, and if you expect to see bad things from particular people, you will see them.

Like prejudice, the issue of discrimination is fuzzy round the edges. A judge recently ruled that it was fair for insurance companies to charge higher premiums to professional women (the case was brought by a dentist) than professional men. Is this discrimination? The case turned on whether women had more time off work than men because of sickness. They do. The answer to that, which was not heeded, is that because of discrimination against women in the labour market, the jobs women get tend to be the kind where illness is almost welcomed as a reason for staying at home. In this way, it may look as though women take more time off work because they are women. A comparison might help here. Students pay higher motor insurance premiums than other people. This could say something about students in general, or it could be that students who can afford cars are often spoiled brats, and spoiled brats are the dangerous ones in cars. There are other difficult situations of the same general kind, which may or may not constitute discrimination. However, for our purposes, the damaging kinds of discrimination are by and large clear to fair-minded people.We have also taken the line that there is no reason for unfair discrimination other than prejudice. Therefore, it is prejudice rather than discrimination which is basic, and we will deal with the topic accordingly. Sadly, although you can legislate against some forms of discrimination, you cannot legislate against its root cause, prejudice.

The causes of prejudice

All the readers of this book will know at least a little of what Jewish people in Europe suffered during the 1930s and 40s. That suffering was only a chapter in a series of sufferings, making up the long history of Jewish persecution. After World War II, there was an attempt to work out why many people are anti-Semitic. One of the most important results of this study was the finding that people who were prejudiced against Jews were not just prejudiced against Jews; they were prejudiced against other minority groups as well. Put simply, you cannot consider anti-Semitism by itself, it is part of a general tendency to be prejudiced. This general tendency to be prejudiced was itself shown to be part of a more general personality type. This type of personality was marked not only by its level of prejudice but also by its concern with authority, requiring submission from subordinates and giving submission to bosses. People with this personality type saw everything, not just people, in black and white terms! They were *intolerant of ambiguity*.

You can try a little experiment of your own to test this. Show a projector slide well out of focus. Ask the person you are with to guess what the picture represents. Then bring the slide a little more into focus, ask them to change their guess if they want to, bring it more into focus, and so on. Some people are prepared to make a guess when the slide is still very much out of focus, and then will be reluctant to change their guess even when the slide is clear enough to make it obvious that their guess is wrong. These are the people who show intolerance of ambiguity. You can probably see how people with this sort of personality type are attracted to one or other of the disciplined services, although the ambiguities of the police role itself will no doubt cause them some grief once they are in it.

The extent to which authoritarian personalities are born or shaped is unclear. It is better to think of them as shaped, and there is some evidence which points in this direction. But even if you do not have an authoritarian personality, you can still be shaped to be prejudiced by simple learning, in the same way that you learn any other attitude, simply by being exposed to the unchallenged views of parents or friends, or being actually rewarded for repeating them. If you hear your family say prejudiced things and your family nods when you say them, you have the basis for prejudice at some level.

What follows is a true story. A boy was told by his father that the trouble with black people is that they smell bad. Since this was in a town where there were virtually no black people around, there was no immediate chance of putting the matter to the test. The boy's first bus ride sitting next to a black person was thus a voyage of discovery. It led to the conclusion that not all black people smell bad. The trouble with prejudice learned in this simple way is that if there had been a choice of seats, the boy would probably not have sat down next to the black person in the first place, and would have continued to believe what he had been told. Another disadvantage of simple learning is that it may lead to the perception of what was expected. If the crucial bus ride had been taken on a hot day, the boy's nose, working hard, might have detected sweat, and his prejudice would have been confirmed. The smell of equally sweaty white people on the bus would, of course, pass unnoticed.

A depressing view of one of the major origins of prejudice comes from the work of Henri Tajfel and his colleagues. This showed that just dividing a group into two sub-groups led to people thinking that people in their own group (the in-group) were better than people in the other group (the out-group). There is inter-regiment rivalry in the army, even though the regiments are supposed to be on the same side in a war. There is inter-force and inter-division rivalry in the police service. The British in their hearts think they are better than the French, even though there is an alliance between the countries. The French know they are wrong!

When you last went to a pantomime, the odds are that the star of the show encouraged a shouting match between those sitting on one side of the central aisle and those sitting on the other side. Even just dividing the audience in this way sows the seeds of mild prejudice against the other lot, but encouraging them to outshout each other puts the icing on it. In a series of unsettling experiments on boys in summer camps, the social psychologist Muzafar Sherif (1966) showed that he could make the boys hate each other simply by getting them to engage in competitive games. To restate, simply dividing people into groups invites prejudice. Then to get the groups to compete with each other makes matters worse.

Let us consider the case of football supporters. Chelsea supporters heartily dislike Fulham supporters even though, at the time of writing, the teams play in different divisions of the football league (social categorization only: they are identifiable clubs). However, they hate Spurs supporters more (social categorizaton plus competition: they play each other regularly). There is an interesting study to be done on the effects of promotion and relegation on supporter hatreds. The prediction would be that hatreds decrease when the teams are no longer in the same division. The decrease would be greatest among teams promoted out of the same division as their rivals and least in a team demoted out of the same division, because frustration also increases aggressive prejudice (a theory we have not dealt with in this chapter, but a useful contributory factor to bear in mind).

The relevant research on football supporters has not yet been done, but the different factors contributing to prejudice (social categorization, competition and frustration) are well enough established for us to be pretty sure of our ground here. In the Sherif experiment, making the boys take part in cooperative games defused the situation in a matter of days. This is an important result. If competing groups can be induced to cooperate in a task where neither group can achieve success alone, prejudice can be overcome or reduced – at least until the competition starts again.

Alf Garnett was Johnny Speight's loud-mouthed central character in the television comedy series 'Till Death Us Do Part' (and more recently 'In Sickness and in Health'). Alf hated minority groups. One of the reasons for this was that he was a fairly authoritarian personality. He expected obedience from his wife, daughter and son-in-law. He himself was submissive to people in authority. Opposing views were dismissed with contempt (intolerance of ambiguity). However, another reason for Alf's prejudice was to do with status. He is a loud-mouthed, boorish, bald, ageing West Ham football club supporter. He can regard himself as top dog in nothing except being white and male, and so he stresses those attributes. He places great emphasis on the superiority of those attributes because it improves his own status and self-esteem. As the social psychologist Gordon Allport noted:

> The easiest idea to sell anyone is that he is better than someone else. The appeal of the Ku Klux Klan and racist agitators rests on this type of salesmanship. Snobbery is a way of clutching at one's status, and it is common, perhaps more common, among those who are low on the ladder. By turning their attention to unfavoured out-groups they are able to derive from the comparison a modicum of self-esteem (Allport 1954).

Although we have given only the bare bones of theories of prejudice, we think we have pointed to some important general principles. People are prejudiced:

- because of the kind of basic personality which they possess
- because of what they have learned or been encouraged to repeat
- because the sheer division of people into 'us' and 'them' devalues 'them' and overvalues 'us'
- because when competition between groups takes place, hostility against the out-group is likely to occur.

The basic tone of the research is not hopeful for easy solutions of inter-group prejudice and discrimination. Until people are 'colour blind', ethnic social categorization will take place. When black and white people are seen to be competing for the same jobs, this too makes things worse. The police service *does* appeal to authoritarian personalities, because command and obedience are valued principles for them.

Before leaving the description of basic research on prejudice, we look at the aspect of the issue which provides a more optimistic slant on the topic.

Attitudes and actions

The relationship between attitudes and actions is a complicated one. One of the earliest studies in prejudice took place when a psychologist found that restaurateurs who said on the phone that they wouldn't serve Chinese people often did serve them when they turned up at the restaurant. A racist white man might wish to attack all black people, but will restrain himself when it comes to black men over six feet tall. Similarly, creating a social climate in which discrimination is against the norm will reduce the amount of obvious discrimination.

An important study of this type of effect was carried out in the Pocohontas coalfield of West Virginia. There, black and white miners developed a lifestyle which seemed on the face of it very inconsistent. There was much friendly contact between black and white miners while they were working underground. However, in the mining town itself, there was much more social segregation between black and white miners. What is the explanation for this? It is that above ground the social pressures were towards segregation, whereas underground they were towards friendly integration, presumably because they relied on each other for their safety at work. The social pressures were critical, as they so often are (see Chapter 6).

This gives hope that creating a social climate in which discrimination is unacceptable in the police service can work to reduce levels of discrimination. There is some suggestion from the officers in the Policy Studies Institute study of the Metropolitan Police that racist talk and racist actions did not necessarily go together. One quotation from an experienced police officer illustrates the point neatly:

> I was talking to a policeman not long ago, one of those who says he hates black people, they're the scum of the earth and all of those things. I said to him 'Suppose you're on a street and two skinheads are doing over a black man, putting the boot in, what would you do?' 'You know what I would do', he said. 'Tell me what you would do, would you intervene?' 'Of course I would', he said. 'Well, what would you do, would you join in kicking the black man?' 'Of course I wouldn't', he said, 'I would come to his aid and sort out the skinheads.' 'Well then', I said, 'when you say you hate blacks, you don't mean it, you're just going through a phase.' It's a recognized thing, you know, that people do go through phases like that.

It is clear from the Policy Studies Institute research and after any amount of contact that there is racism among police officers just as there is in the communities from which they, and we, come. We find denials of this fact by some senior officers naïve or dishonest. To some extent racism is moderated by professional standards, but this cannot be relied on, in the police or any other professional organization. Even small degrees of racism can be shown in subtle discriminations, refusals to help, indifference to problems, and so on.

We return later to a statement of why we regard the psychology of racial prejudice as important and why we think it is important to have a major offensive against racism in the police. If it is not forth-coming, we foresee nothing but a difficult and violent future in police–ethnic community relations. The fact that the police have to be at the centre of the problem is unfair. Police officers carry an extra burden – racist behaviour by them has more scope for expression, the arenas in which it can be expressed are very important, and racism is more likely to be alleged against the police than other professions. A policeman's lot ... (not to mention a policewoman's).

How can you be fair in an unfair world?

Imagine a saintly young man or woman who joins the police force. He or she loves everyone, is motivated by ideals of service, and wants to be even-handed in the administration of the law. How can it be done? The officer is patrolling a prosperous suburb, and comes across a young black man dressed in grubby T-shirt and jeans. What should the officer do? If the decision is to stop and question the young man, the objection could be raised that a white youth simi-larly dressed would not have been stopped, so it was unfair. If the decision is not to stop the youth, the objection is that the officer knows that no black people live in the area, so it is justified to stop the black youth not because he is black, but because he is a stranger to the area. If the white youth could be so easily identified as a stranger on the scene, he too would have been stopped. It is not the police officer's fault that skin colour is a particularly easy marker for strangeness in an area. (Or for strangeness in being found driving a luxury car. A black rugby league star exchanged his car for a more modest one because he was forever getting stopped by the police.)

It gets even more difficult for our young (W)PC Saintly. The rea-son why no black people live in the posh suburb is largely that black people get a raw deal in employment and education. So the reason you can identify the black youth as a stranger is because, through a history of discrimination, people like him cannot afford to live in an area like that. By stopping the black youth Saintly would be adding the insult of a stop to the injury of long term discrimination against his people. The problem was graphically described in a rather differ-ent form by an experienced RUC inspector. The Irish setting has some advantages as an example here, because it lacks the emotive overtones of race. (Perhaps it should not, but it does.) One RUC inspector asked in desperation how he could be fair in nationalist areas. RUC officers have been (until very recently) in much more danger, on or off duty, in nationalist than in loyalist areas. By accepting friendly overtures in a nationalist area, by giving information and passing the time of day, visibility and vulnerability is increased. By not taking these actions, officers are cutting themselves off even further from the nationalist community they seek to serve. Is the RUC officer to behave in the same way in all areas and decrease personal safety, or behave in different ways and be guilty of partiality to one community?

The same kind of problem exists in black communities concerning the policing of cannabis use. The drug has a different meaning for Anglicans and Rastafarians. Does the officer enforce the letter of the law evenly, and thus ignore these differences of significance, or enforce according to the significance, and thus unevenly in fact? There are no easy answers, and we think appeals to community policing fudge issues like these. What we have tried to do in this section is to say that a racism-free police force would still not be out of the wood. A police force composed entirely of Saintlys still has some important and non-obvious operational decisions to make.

Why the problem needs urgent and radical attention

When we described theories of prejudice earlier, we did so from the perspective of the police service. The social categorization into us (police) and them (Blacks), with competition as an added element is the recipe for prejudice against black people among police officers. It is also the recipe for prejudice against police officers among black people. The same characteristics of prejudice (not making enough differentiation among members of the out-group, devaluing them, etc.) work both ways. That means a vicious spiral, with prejudiced blacks behaving in ways which confirm prejudiced police officers in their views, and so on, with the misunderstandings growing ever more frequent and painful. One police officer we know said he dreaded stopping cars with black drivers because they will believe that the stop was based on race and be awkward. By behaving as though it is, and believing that, the wedge between the groups is driven farther in. Another example of the consequences of the wedge comes from an officer of whose integrity and lack of racial bias we are totally convinced from long acquaintance. He made the point that some black people were telling their friends that they had been beaten up while in police custody, because not to say you had been beaten up would have been tantamount to saying that you had been acting as an informer.

It is difficult to avoid the conclusion that this vicious spiral of prejudice and discrimination is such that only the large scale recruitment and promotion of non-white police officers will help, so that divisions into the police and the policed cannot so easily be made on simple ethnic grounds. The alternative, of positive discrimination in favour of black people by police officers, is as unrealistic as a general solution as it would be politically unacceptable.

If you were a racist when you started this book, you will almost certainly still be a racist when, or rather if, you finish it. You will reject out of hand the need for major recruitment and promotion of black police officers. By doing so, you will be contributing, we think, to making policing an unnecessarily violent and difficult task in ethnic communities in the next half-century.

Women officers, recruitment and image

It would be wrong to end the chapter without some reference to the position of women police officers, and to discrimination among police officers more generally. This is one of those difficult areas where it is hard to know where fairness ends and discrimination begins. For example, women officers are clearly on average physically less strong than male officers, but do they have other attributes which make the need for force less likely when they are involved? Your answer will help to determine whether you think women officers are discriminated against. We take two things to be clear.

- Women are expected by men to take sexual talk and horseplay as part of their initiation into police culture. This only comes to public notice when it goes very much too far.
- Recent developments resulting in much greater numbers of women recruits into the police service have raised the issue of whether the criteria of selection for women officers are or should be the same as those for men.

Our impression is that this issue has been raised in one of two ways. The first is that women are selected for characteristics of 'femininity', like social charm, gentleness, concern for the young. They will then be directed into particular specialisms, notably juvenile liaison and community relations, and be expected to perform general police duties in a distinctive way. This type of approach is the one favoured by and reflected in television series about women police officers (*The Gentle Touch*, *Juliet Bravo*).

The second way we see recruitment proceeding is the opposite of the first. That is to say, women recruits must show the same attributes as their male counterparts, but must show them to a greater extent, to compensate for being women. In this way, women would be accepted into the service if they showed a preference for action, discipline and determination, but to an extent that cancels out their being women. As the old car hire advertisement claimed, Number 2 tries harder. If being a woman makes you Number 2, you have to be even more of a stereotypical police officer to make up for this. You may recall that in our first chapter, we noted that women officers were less convinced than men of the value of psychology for police work. We feel that this is linked to the 'Number 2 tries harder' theory. To be successful women officers must be even harder-headed than men. Rejecting the 'soft' subjects, like psychology, must be seen as one way of doing this. If we are at least partly correct in our impressions about the selection of women police officers, there is room for improvement and more general recognition of the proper and non-discriminatory recruitment and deployment of women officers.

This final paragraph is a brief attempt to draw your attention to issues which would merit much more detailed attention in a larger book than this one. Criteria for selection, training, assessment and promotion of officers are little investigated, and yes, they could properly belong in a chapter on prejudice and discrimination.

One study showed that it was *social conformity* which distinguished successful from unsuccessful male applicants for the police service. Interestingly, different criteria were important for the success of women applicants. Most informed discussions of this group of topics are not complimentary about the present state of, for example, performance assessment. But there, unhappily, our discussion must rest. Just talk to your colleagues about your experience. What was it about you that led you to be recruited in the first place and assessed as you have been since then? Do your colleagues share your feelings and experiences?

Review notes

Prejudice is an attitude, discrimination a behaviour. Prejudice comes from the mere division of people into distinguishable groups, personality factors in the prejudiced person, competition between groups and feelings of frustration.

Prejudiced attitudes do not always translate into discriminatory actions. Social climates determine whether this will happen. Given the important social position of the police officer, discriminatory behaviour can have severe direct impact on the course of people's lives and cause hatred of the police. How not to be discriminatory is not always obvious, even when there is no trace of prejudice involved. Discrimination can develop into a vicious spiral with, for example, police and ethnic minorities becoming increasingly alienated from each other. We strongly advocate recruitment of police officers from ethnic minorities. This will bring its own problems, but will blur the most obvious contrasts between police and policed.

There is considerable scope for discrimination against women officers in the police service. Some women officers over-compensate by becoming, in their attitudes, more like policemen than policewomen.

References

Allport, G.W. (1954) *The Nature of Prejudice*. Reading, Mass.: Addison-Wesley.
Sherif, M. (1966) *In Common Predicament: Social Psychology of Intergroup Conflict and Cooperation*. Boston: Houghton-Mifflin.
Smith, D.J. and Gray, J. (1983) *Police and People in London. IV: The Police in Action*. London: Policy Studies Institute.

Further reading

Aronson, E. (1984) *The Social Animal*, 4th ed. New York: Freeman.
Baron, R.A. and Byrne, D. (1984) *Social Psychology: Understanding Human Interaction*, 4th ed. Boston: Allyn & Bacon.
Turner, J.C. and Giles, H. (eds) (1981) *Intergroup Behaviour*. Oxford: Basil Blackwell.

Chapter 9

Family Disputes and Crisis Intervention Techniques

Many of the incidents to which police officers are called are crises of some kind: a domestic disturbance; someone falling victim to a serious crime or learning that a relative has died. It is almost invariably a police officer who is called to the scene of incidents of this kind, and his or her actions will go a long way towards determining the outcome of the crisis, both physically and emotionally. While some studies have suggested that incidents of this type may not be regarded by many officers as 'real' police work, the fact remains that the public expect a police officer to deal with them efficiently, and that they are so frequent that they form a large proportion of the experiences which people have of the police, and hence attitudes towards them.

Some research has suggested that more than half the calls received by the police are requests for service of some kind. Other researchers have suggested that police officers are often expected to be '24-hour social workers' as well as acting as law-enforcers or peace-keepers. Discussing whether or not police officers *should* be taking on this role is outside our scope. So long as police officers are called upon to deal with important and troubled times in people's lives, we feel that an understanding of crisis intervention techniques will be of benefit. In the USA, most police officers undergo formal training in this area, usually provided by a psychologist. However, in Britain and in many other countries, knowledge is expected to be gained from experienced colleagues, who may or may not be good at dealing with such incidents.

Experience is a good teacher, but not everyone benefits equally from its lessons. Psychologists do have advice and knowledge which will supplement the good practice of experienced colleagues.

Such knowledge may help officers in their dealings with unpredictable, potentially explosive situations, which often involve a threat to the officer's personal safety. The successful resolution of a crisis may also mean that an officer is less likely to be called back to the scene, as might well happen if the incident is handled ineffectively. In pure personal efficiency terms, effective crisis handling will pay off.

Most police officers would agree that prevention of crime is as important a goal as the detection of crime, and successful intervention in crises offers an opportunity to prevent crime. Assaults, child abuse, criminal damage and so on may well all be the result of inadequate attempts to resolve crises. We would also remind the reader that in half of all murder cases the victim was either a relative or acquaintance of the murderer. Although the public may have a fear of being murdered by a complete stranger in a dark deserted street, the reality is that the home is a much more dangerous place. Home is where the heart is but it is also where the murderer is. As we point out later, a large number of assaults occur in homes to which the police have been called more than once.

We start with a brief outline of the development of crisis theory. In 1942 the Coconut Grove fire in Boston Massachusetts claimed the lives of 493 people. Eric Lindemann, a psychiatrist, played an active role in helping both the survivors and the relations of victims. This led to one of the most important contributions to the understanding of the grief process. Lindemann was able to show that mourning progresses through a series of identifiable stages leading to final acceptance and resolution of the crisis. Perhaps even more importantly, Lindemann suggested that a whole host of people in the community are in a position to help the recently bereaved and in this they may forestall psychological difficulties later in life. This lead was followed by Gerald Caplan, who suggested that poorly handled crises or transitions led to mental illness in a large number of cases – but that crises also offered the opportunity for personal development. He quickly established the importance of both personal and social resources in determining whether crises would lead to an improvement or a decline in the person's mental health.

Around this time, one of the first suicide prevention centres was established in Los Angeles. Contemplating suicide was seen as an obvious sign that an individual was unable to cope with some life crisis, and the centre was established with a primary objective of saving lives. It was recognized that for some age groups suicide was frequent and also that a suicide could affect the mental health of surviving loved ones. Many of the so-called 'Suicide Prevention Centers' in the USA were able to provide assistance to people who were experiencing a wide variety of crises. The Centers came to offer support for 24 hours of the day to anyone who experienced a problem and felt they needed immediate assistance. In Britain, organizations like the Samaritans now assume similar responsibilities.

The central theme running through all these developments was preventing what was undoubtedly a traumatic event in the life of an individual from developing into a long term behavioural problem. Long term intensive help may not be needed if appropriate assistance could be offered as soon as possible after the crisis had developed. It was also seen that police officers were in the front line of preventative mental health care and could be a valuable resource.

A crisis can be seen as a temporary state of distress and disorganization usually characterized by an individual's inability to cope with the particular problem using their usual coping or problemsolving techniques. The crisis can be seen as a danger because it threatens to overwhelm the person. However, any crisis is also an *opportunity* which may allow the person to develop more effective coping strategies and thus allow an individual to function at a higher level than before the event. Donna Aguilera and Janice Messick describe the situation as follows:

> A person in crisis is at a turning point. He faces problems that he cannot readily solve by using the coping mechanisms that have worked for him before ... A person in this situation feels helpless – he is caught in a state of great emotional upset and feels unable to take action *on his own* to solve the problem.

Karl Slaikeu suggests that the process of crisis intervention can be broken down into two phases: first order intervention or 'psychological first aid', and second order intervention or 'crisis therapy'. While the latter may take weeks or months, the former may take only a few minutes. Psychological first aid, like physical first aid, needs to be invoked immediately and, most importantly, needs to be invoked by those who have the initial contact with the sufferer. Most often, this will be a family member or friends. If not, it will almost certainly be a police officer.

A number of life events are regarded as so grave that we would all agree that they represent crises. Despite the fact that some individuals may be more hardy than others, such events as a sudden death or suffering a rape will typically mean crisis. However, almost any sudden change or unanticipated event can lead an individual to feel stressed, as you will read in Chapter 12. In many of the stressful events described there a police officer would be on hand. Crises and the police are frequent companions.

Domestic disturbances

Attending domestic disputes is probably one of the least favourite activities of police officers on duty. William Patton identified a number of reasons why this might be so. He suggested that the call is often made by a citizen who has a vested interest in what action an officer takes (for example, a wife who wants her husband locking up). The calls also tend to be time consuming, as the officer must go through the background of the incident and its participants. Domestic disturbances are difficult because they are ambiguous, especially as regards the balance of responsibility.

Although ambiguity and unpredictability are important considerations, Al Goldstein and his colleagues have pointed out that the two most important aspects of these calls are that they will involve people who are emotionally upset or even mentally disturbed and the officer's personal safety must be at risk. It has been estimated that almost one third of all assaults on police officers occur while attending domestic disputes. However, not all officers are equally at risk. For example, Paul Horstman suggested that the probability that an officer will be assaulted is high when his interpersonal skills and appropriate use of authority are low.

In order to help police officers to deal more effectively with this difficult type of call, many forces in the USA have recently introduced training programmes. The most commonly cited example involves the work of Morton Bard with New York City officers. Here a number of selected officers were specially trained to deal with crisis calls. The training involved lectures, role playing exercises, and so on.

The training did not lead to a decrease in the number of calls received. It did result in fewer assaults and injuries sustained by police officers, compared to a neighbouring area where officers had not received specialist training. Bard's approach has been criticized because it set up specialist squads of officers to deal with specific incidents, rather than having all officers in the area trained in crisis intervention techniques, but this does not alter the fact that the approach did have benefits and would presumably have benefits at least as great if all officers had been trained.

John Driscoll was able to evaluate the effects of a crisis intervention programme introduced in Lewisville (USA). When questioned some time after the training, the police officers who had been trained confirmed that the training had given them an increased understanding of family problems, and they were more accepted by members of the public. The officers also reported that they tended to use less force and were generally more effective. The change was also recognized by the citizens who had called in the police. They reported a greater rapport between themselves and the officers involved, leading to an increased level of satisfaction with and regard for the police.

Perhaps one of the most exhaustive evaluations of crisis intervention training is reported by Donald Dutton and Brian Levens. They found that officers trained in these techniques were significantly different from untrained officers in a number of areas:

- They were more likely to negotiate the settlement of a problem and to refer the case to an outside agency.
- They were more likely to use long term strategies to reduce the conflict.
- They were more satisfied with their specialist training than were officers who received traditional training.
- They reported a greater feeling of accomplishment and were more willing to get involved in domestic crisis calls.
- They reported decreases in violence and the use of force compared to other officers.
- They reported increases in the public's level of satisfaction with their actions.

Many other workers have been involved in training police officers in this kind of work. Although not all have evaluated effectiveness thoroughly, most point to improved relationships, both between the police and members of the public, and between the police and other social services agencies.

Jeffrey Luckett and Karl Slaikeu (1984) point out that there is considerable variation in the style of training programmes. Some rely on simulation and videotape feedback, some give broad procedural guidelines, while others offer quite detailed instructions to be followed when dealing with crisis situations. However, almost all the training programmes concentrate on two areas, namely:

- the police officer using his or her authority to calm intensely charged situations
- the police officer taking steps to reduce the physical danger.

The concentration on the second area is not surprising given the greater threat that North American officers face compared to their British counterparts.

We are particularly impressed by the writings of Luckett and Slaikeu, who draw on the concept of 'psychological first aid' and the work of Al Goldstein. They offer concrete proposals to aid officers dealing with crisis situations and the remainder of this chapter will draw heavily on their work.

We introduced the notion of 'psychological first aid' earlier and this seems to be an appropriate point to discuss the notion more fully. Slaikeu suggests that the chief goal of psychological first aid is to re-establish immediate coping. However, three subgoals are identified:

Providing support. This can range from 'being there' to expressing concern and reinforcing the others' strengths.

Reducing lethality. Reducing the risk of physical injury and thereby saving the lives of those embroiled and those trying to help.

Providing linkage to helping resources. Bearing in mind that crises often mean that a person's normal coping strategies are inadequate, the task of the psychological first aider is to point the person in the direction of an appropriate helping resource. This can be something as practical as giving the phone number of a social services department, victim support scheme or some other agency which can better deal with the problem on a long term basis.

This gives general guiding principles about what to do, but it is not very clear about how to do it. Any mere book presentation of how to do it is a poor second-best to experiencing the techniques in training, but Luckett and Slaikeu do spell out the steps helpful in achieving the three major purposes, and these are set out in detail. They suggest five steps which can serve as a set of guidelines for dealing with the full range of crisis calls. Their classification follows.

1. Approaching the scene

It is vital that an officer is prepared mentally when approaching a crisis situation. This can take the form of reviewing previous experience, anticipating the unexpected and thinking through a provisional course of action. A large part of this preparation is concerned with safety and the neutralization of possible threats.

Goldstein suggests that this is not simply a matter of the removal of obvious weapons, but also of considering where the officer should be positioned (for example, not near windows or stairs) or always having one's partner in view, even if he or she is in a different room.

2. Making psychological contact

After an officer has minimized the risk of physical harm, he or she can start to reduce tensions and defuse the situation. Goldstein suggests that an officer should try to present an image of 'non-hostile authority'. The uniform is a symbol of authority, though an over-zealous use of this authority may well make the situation worse. It is important that the officer achieves a balance between being too harsh or too soft. Goldstein offers a number of suggestions for 'calming down' the situation. These include *conversational methods* such as:

Showing understanding. Empathy is one of the most important attributes that any helper can show. In the case of police crisis intervention this is simply letting the distraught person know that the officer understands or can appreciate what the person is going through. This should not go so far as supporting one side in a dispute or telling an individual that they are justified: rather the officer should simply show an understanding of the way the person is feeling.

Modelling calm behaviour. The officer who appears tense, nervous and hostile will make a fraught situation worse. However, if the officer arrives on the scene calm and collected, a reassuring presence is available to the people involved. This calming can be achieved verbally and non-verbally through facial expression, posture and gesture (see Chapter 2).

Reassuring. This step involves the officer in passing on his or her own calmness to other participants. Simple reassurance, where realistic, in the form of 'this will work itself out' or assuring the person that many other people have gone through the same experience may be helpful.

Encouraging talking and using distractions. Simply getting a person to talk will generally help to defuse a hostile situation. The officer should try to reinforce appropriate behaviour (by talking calmly about the situation) but to discourage inappropriate reactions like shouting and screaming. In fact Goldstein suggests that an officer should learn to recognize when it is better for the person to talk about the incident itself and when it may be better to get the person to talk about other things. Which strategy to adopt can be determined by watching the person's reactions when talking about the incident or when giving background information. Some people will feel a need to talk while others may, at least for the time being, prefer to be distanced from the event. In fact Goldstein suggests that an effective way of calming distraught people is to divert their attention from the incident. Suggestions about achieving this include asking the person to get the officer a drink of water!

Using humour. It is a well-established and useful fact that people cannot experience two contradictory emotions at the same time. Therefore matching aggression and anger with humour *can* be a good way of defusing tension, although a very risky one. In many circumstances humour would be offensive, and the right conditions for the joke have to be gauged carefully.

It is recognized that these conversational methods of calming people down may not always be successful and Goldstein suggests two further, *assertive* methods.

Repeating and 'outshouting'. Often a person in crisis may be so angry or confused as to be virtually unaware of what is happening around them. These people will rarely respond to the methods listed above, so the officer will need to repeat what is being said several times before the message gets through. If the person is shouting loudly the officer may have to resort to 'outshouting' the person before they start to listen.

Using physical restraint. Goldstein acknowledges that with some people all the above techniques may prove unsuccessful and it may prove necessary to restrain the person physically.

The old rule of using only such force as is necessary is equally or especially true in domestic disturbances. Many officers will be aware of how quickly one party in the dispute can change from demanding police action to attacking the officer when he or she tries to arrest the offending spouse! Two alternative tactics are advocated.

Using trusted others. Sometimes the officer may not be the best person to deal with a crisis. The delivery of a death message for example may be made easier for the recipient if the officer is accompanied by a friend or neighbour of the bereaved person. This method can also be used for someone who dislikes or distrusts police officers, but who may perhaps listen to a priest or relative.

Temporarily ignoring the person. In some circumstances it may be appropriate or necessary to ignore a hysterical person completely. Behaviourist theorists in psychology tell us that any action which is not 'reinforced' is likely to 'extinguish'. In other words, if the person is not getting attention by screaming, he or she may stop and try another tactic. There may also be other circumstances which necessitate the officer ignoring a hysterical person (for example, a screaming mother whose child is bleeding from a head wound).

It is largely through experience that a police officer will learn which of these methods to adopt in any given situation, although it is important to remember that officers who are not aware of the whole range of possible techniques will *not* gain the full benefits of experience. You cannot learn about things you never try. An officer who is well versed in the different options will be better able to deal with the diverse incidents which go collectively under the heading of 'crises'. Although some of the options are common sense, and sound like common sense, the officer having the whole range to choose from is an ideal not always found in reality.

3. Examining dimensions of the problem

Just like the 'physical first aider' a crisis worker needs to decide which aspects of the problem require immediate attention and which can be delayed. The intervening officer must decide whether the person is dangerous to themselves or others; whether the person can cope with the problem alone; whether action should be directed to any criminal offence committed. Goldstein suggests a range of questions and strategies to gather information including:

Open-ended questions. These allow the person to explain the problem in his or her own way: 'Tell me how you get on with each other when things are going well.'
Closed-ended questions. These allow the person to answer only yes or no, which enables the officer to take charge of the interaction: 'Are there any children involved?'
Listening. This is an obvious enough strategy though the officer must show by non-verbal means that he or she is attending.
Restatement of content. Repeating the story in the officer's own words reassures the person that they have been understood.
Reflection of feelings. The officer should demonstrate that he or she understands not only what is said, but how the person feels about it.
Selective inattention and use of silence. The officer may show that he or she is interested in some aspects of what the person is saying,

by reinforcing some things and not commenting on irrelevancies.
Self-dislosure and use of immediacy. People generally tend to disclose their fears and feelings when the person with whom they are talking discloses similar information. However, Goldstein warns that an officer who reveals too much about him or herself may thereby lose the person's respect. (Imagine your reaction if your doctor told you that she wasn't feeling very well either.) The officer should also try to comment favourably on the positive actions which the person has been trying to take.
Confrontation. This is a skilled interview technique where the officer may wish to point out discrepancies or inconsistencies in what the person says or does.
Demanding. In the case of a hostile or dangerous person, the police officer may use his or her authority to command the person to do certain things there and then.

4. Exploring possible solutions

Although by definition crises arise because a person's normal coping mechanisms are ineffective, Luckett and Slaikeu suggest that the officer should try to get the person to think about possible ways of resolving the problem. Indeed, simple solutions offered may well be rejected. People are much more likely to try things they suggest themselves.

5. Taking concrete action

Provided a solution presents little danger, a crime has not been committed and the person involved is not too disturbed, Luckett and Slaikeu suggest a police officer's intervention could facilitate improvement of a situation in three ways:

Mediation. For a police officer dealing with, say, a domestic dispute, mediation is often accepted. The officer can clarify points of disagreement and encourage the suggestion of possible ways round them. The basic approach in mediation is to assist the disputants in arriving at their own solutions.
Negotiation. By negotiation, Luckett and Slaikeu mean actually considering solutions or compromises and helping people to choose between options. Negotiation is thus a more directive approach than mediation, and may involve assisting direct negotiation between the disputants.
Counselling. This is seen as the most facilitative response, with an

officer actually giving advice on how the problem may be resolved or actually making a referral to another agency, like a victim support scheme.

Luckett and Slaikeu suggest that if the danger is high or the person is unable to help him or herself, then the officer may take a *directive* stance to control the situation or ensure a particular outcome. This may involve arbitration by a third party, arrest of someone or taking them to a psychiatric hospital.

Following up

Although a police officer may often not have the time to follow up all the calls which he or she may have to deal with, the people concerned could be asked to inform the officer about how things go. Only by doing some sort of check back can the officer ever know whether the steps taken helped. This could be undertaken by someone other than a police officer, especially if a referral has been suggested. A small amount of time spent doing some sort of follow up may also serve to cut down the number of repeat calls to an unresolved problem. Research in America has shown that some 90 per cent of aggravated domestic assaults occurred in households to which the police had been called at least once previously. However, if police officers do allow themselves to become involved in people's problems in this way, they will need appropriate training and support from their forces.

Real police work

We are aware than this chapter may appear controversial, especially as regards the notion of whether crisis intervention is 'real' police work. As we stated earlier, the fact is that the public do turn to the police and expect problems to be dealt with. Luckett and Slaikeu suggest that there are a number of ways in which antagonism to this type of work may be reduced.

Notable among these is the idea that police officers themselves should be involved in the design and implementation of training programmes, rather than have outsiders come in and lecture for a few hours. Emphasis should be placed on the positive benefits associated with effective crisis management, such as reducing the amount of time spent on repeat calls and lessening the risk of police injuries. These are benefits which should appeal to more conventional police thinking.

We invite you to read this chapter again the day after you next have to deal with a personal crisis of the kind involved, and to think about the relevance of the issues to that concrete instance. Only a minority of techniques will be relevant to any particular incident, but we suspect you will find that there will be issues you have simply overlooked. Self-assessment of this kind is, we feel, underused in the police service generally. In the case of this chapter, testing out your skills against the specifc points mentioned is probably necessary – both to remember the points in the chapter and to make use of them.

Review notes

Crisis intervention work is an essential component of a great deal of police activity. We have shown that an officer correctly trained in these procedures will have greater control of situations and feel less apprehensive about them. Although we have tended to concentrate on domestic disputes, the principles outlined here are equally applicable to such incidents as suicide threats, serious crime victimization, or delivering death messages. For the police officers themselves, successful crisis intervention work may well mean less time spent on repeat calls, more opportunities to prevent serious crime, and a greater appreciation by people in the community served.

Readers are encouraged to look back over the chapter the day after they are next called upon to intervene in a crisis.

References

Aguilera, D.C. and Messick, J.M. (1978) *Crisis Intervention Theory and Methodology*. St Louis: Mosby.

Bard, M. (1970) *Training Police as Specialists in Family Crisis Intervention*. Washington, DC: National Institute of Law Enforcement and Criminal Justice.

Caplan, G. (1961) *An Approach to Community Mental Health*. New York: Grune and Stratton.

Driscoll, J., Meyer, R.G. and Schanie, C.F. (1973) Training police in family crisis intervenion. *Journal of Applied Behavioural Sciences*, 9, 172–192.

Dutton, D.G. (1981) Training police officers to intervene in domestic violence. In R.B.Stuart (ed.) *Violent Behaviour: Social Learning Approaches to Prediction, Management and Treatment*. New York: Bruner/Maazel.

Dutton, D.G. and Levens, B. (1977) Attitude survey of trained and untrained police officers. *Canadian Police College Journal*, 2, 75–92.

Goldstein, A.P. Monti, P.J., Sardino, T.J. and Green, D.J. (1979) *Police Crisis Intervention*. Elmsland, NY: Pergamon Press.

Hartsman, P.L. (1974) Assaults on police officers: how safe are you? In R.W. Kobetz (ed.) *Crisis Intervention and the Police: Selected Readings*. Gauthersburg, Md: International Association of Chiefs of Police.

Luckett, J.B. and Slaikeu, K.A. (1984) Crisis intervention by police. In K.A. Slaikeu (ed.) *Crisis Intervention: A Handbook for Practice and Research.* Boston: Allyn & Bacon.
Slaikeu, K.A. (ed.) (1984) *Crisis Intervention: A Handbook for Practice and Research.* Boston: Allyn & Bacon.

Further reading

Slaikeu, K.A. (ed.) (1984) *Crisis Intervention: A Handbook for Practice and Research.* Boston: Allyn & Bacon.

Chapter 10

Hostage Taking

Most of the chapters up to this point have dealt with everyday topics of concern to most police officers. This chapter deals with what we hope will be a very rare occurrence for any officer, and one that many may never encounter. We have included the topic for two reasons. First, in a survey about psychology and police work, police officers agreed that hostage-taking was the type of incident in which psychologists could be of most help. Second, we believe that although expert backup will always be called for in hostage situations, the actions of the first officer on the scene will have a major effect on the eventual outcome. Indeed, rapport established with that officer may give him or her an important part to play in the subsequent negotiations.

One obvious problem in giving generalized advice is that there is no such thing as a general situation, there are only specific situations. A father threatening to kill his child is somewhat different from the kidnapping of a group of strangers for political purposes. Neither is similar to the situation where hostages are taken after a robbery goes wrong. Giving a simple 'how to do it' guide is not an option, given the variation in incidents which are subsumed under the heading 'hostage situations'. One danger to which we draw attention, however, is that the police culture, putting a premium on action, may dispose officers to act immediately, rather than play out a possibly protracted waiting game. We hope that the rest of this chapter will give officers some notion of what may be involved in this type of incident, and prepare them for the day when they are first on the scene.

The hostage situation

What is the minimum number of people involved in a hostage situation? If you said two, think again. The *three* people necessary for a hostage situation are captor, hostage and *audience*. The captor wishes to exchange something over which he or she has power for something over which the audience is thought to have control. The reason for stressing that hostage-taking is a 'game' for a minimum of three players is that until the third person agrees to play, there is no game. There have been cases where police officers have simply walked up to captors and disarmed them because they had not recognized the situation as one of hostage-taking, or where officers have walked away from a captor and hostage, thus ending the incident.

This is obviously a risky way of doing things. If the captor does harm the hostage, the officer will feel terrible and be disciplined. But it is not always a crazy option. We would really like to know how many hostage-takings have been nipped in the bud by a terse 'Don't be daft' from a police officer. Another implication of this is that the offer to énd the 'game' should be explicitly made to the captor as often as possible. Hostage-takings may be dragged out longer than they need be simply because no one thought to suggest to the captor that he give up.

Who deals well with hostage situations?

One of the better-known results of police research is that officers vary enormously in their tendency to get themselves into difficult, violent situations. This is illustrated well in the police novels of Joseph Wambaugh, himself a former policeman. Such differences reflect communication skills or lack of them. Communication skills start with noticing things. In hostage situations, like all other situations, you cannot react to something if you have not noticed it in the first place. Skill at sport, work and crafts concerns noticing small signs. Good cricketers see subtleties in the delivery of cricket balls that others do not, sculptors see imperfections in stone, and so on. In the same way, social skills – of which communications is a part – rely on noticing things. You will be aware from your own experience that some people seem so sensitive to moods and tensions that they seem all but psychic. There are others who display all the subtlety of a clog-dancing elephant. Communication skills can be learned, and are the most important thing to know in any fraught situation, including hostage situations. Some key elements of social skills are described in Chapter 2. In the book *Hostage* by Murray Miron and Arnold Goldstein it is made quite clear that the sensitivity and skill of the officer in charge is a prime factor, probably the key factor, in determining the course of a hostage-taking. Other writers have tended to concentrate on personality characteristics of the hostage-taker, but we think that while detailed information about the hostage-taker is important, it is the skill of the officer rather than the diagnostic category of the captor which is more important for a successful outcome. Even the most socially-skilled negotiator needs some guidance, though. The guidelines we give are adapted and shortened from the Miron and Goldstein book.

Guidelines for hostage negotiators

At the outset of a hostage situation, the goals are those of stabilization and containment. All precipitous actions should be avoided. Once this has been achieved, effort should be directed to getting the situation seen as one of problem solving, creating an atmosphere in which compromise is recognized as a major goal. The bargaining style which is usually to be preferred is one of hard compromise. Soft bargaining and forcing are the rocks between which to steer. To stress again our starting position, though, it all depends on the perpetrator.

Attempts should be made to calm the perpetrator by displaying calmness oneself, and avoiding provocation. Being sensitive to non-verbal cues of aggression should allow some idea of when to encourage perpetrators to express their feelings and when to attempt to distract them from the source of their concern.

Building a rapport with the perpetrator may occur naturally with time. Avoid talking down, criticizing, threatening or acting impatiently. Telling him or her about yourself and expressing personal warmth and appreciation of his or her feelings may also be relevant. Development of the rapport will go along with the gathering of information, by asking questions, listening and paraphrasing what the perpetrator has said to show you understand it, including reflecting the feeling it contains, and asking questions to clarify inconsistencies in what is said. Understanding of this kind is a necessary condition of really communicating, and may form the basis of persuasion, because you know the hostage taker's reasoning about his or her situation, and where it is vulnerable or unsure.

Dealing first with smaller issues is a common tactic psychologists use in generating change of view, but in hostage situations, it is not thought good practice to make even the smallest concessions lightly. Conceding small things, and demonstrating that even that is not easy, may temper or remove the larger demands. An important point, again common to many psychologists' tactics, is to understand that facts usually do *not* speak for themselves. Just giving facts is not as persuasive as giving the facts and spelling out the conclusions the facts lead to. Avoid audiences and challenges, try to persuade calmly and gradually. In virtually all hostage situations, realism leads directly to surrender. Factual and rational statements, with their conclusions spelled out, without challenge or threat, will lead to the realization that victory is not possible, but that there are different ways to surrender. As Miron and Goldstein put it:

> Use suggestion, clarification and concretization to make the perpetrator understand better his own intentions, expected gains and likely costs. When the perpetrator presents issues in a global, intangible, irrational or general manner, recast them in specific, tangible, rational terms.

The dynamics of hostage situations

As a rough and ready rule, people's behaviour is changed by its consequences. If something you do results in a state of affairs you like, you are more likely to do it again. Punishment is far more unpredictable in its effects on behaviour than reward. One of the things that is rewarding is simply getting attention. This is well known to good teachers. Very often, being told off is better than being ignored! So it is important to remember in hostage situations (those involving family members in particular) that captors may be enjoying a level of attention they have never had before, and that in itself might be enough to sustain the situation. Many of the people who take hostages are, to put it crudely, failures in life. They are often those who cannot get the world to take notice of them. This means (and we expand on this later) that their expectations of success are low, and that minor concessions may be enough to end the affair. It also means that media attention is a heady experience to them. Cutting off the attention from the captor by one means or another (switching off power, getting the media to cooperate in not covering the event, and so on), is one technique for making the occasion less exciting for the captor.

Miron and Goldstein, in their survey of hostage-takings, include cases where a mother and child were released in exchange for cigarettes, and where an aircraft hijacking ended with the acceptance of beer and sandwiches as a substitute for political demands. They make the point that concentration on the immediate physical demands of the hostage-taker rather than the more abstract demands (such as the release of prisoners, personal immunity and weapons) serves to bring the negotiation into an achievable area. Because hostage-takers are often accustomed to failing, to reality falling below what is desired, the tactic is successful surprisingly often. Another of the consequences of this is that the promise of attention after the hostage is released may be valuable in helping a disturbed captor to have something other than neglect to look forward to. If attention is seen as the 'reward' for releasing the hostage, this may ease matters.

A second point about rewards is that the captor has only one bargaining chip. Harm to or loss of the hostage removes the only power he or she has got, though this obviously applies less in the case of religious fanaticism, where the captor does not mind dying. The lesson from this is that unless there is a powerful reason for speedy intervention, delay until specialist help is available will do no huge harm. In fact, delay is helpful. Imagine the hostage as a bargaining chip of a particular value. The perceived value of the chip can diminish in one of two ways. If the audience does not rush to satisfy the captor's demands, the hostage will be seen as not worth dashing about for. Further, the hostage only has any value while the captor is still prepared to inflict harm. Every hour that passes makes the threat of harm less plausible, and gives more chance for the captor to see the hostage as a real person, and be less inclined towards harm.

The psychology of hostages

The change in the way in which hostages see their situation is both fascinating in itself and of practical importance for those dealing with hostage situations. It was known long before the recent spate of kidnaps that there was a tendency for some people under the control of others to develop attachments to them and to imitate them. Examples of this come from situations as diverse as the schoolboy crush on the female teacher and the concentration camp inmate's behaviour towards guards. In the context of hostage taking, it is known as the 'Stockholm syndrome' after an incident in that city. Here hostages were held for several days in a bank vault by trapped would-be bank robbers. The hostages expressed a strong attachment to their captors after release, even refusing to give evidence against them. There are good reasons why the hostage may develop such a bond, which have been spelled out by Ian McKenzie as follows.

- The hostage's interests coincide with those of the captor, because the hostage's freedom depends upon the captor's demands being met.
- Groups formed in harsh circumstances stick together with a strange ferocity (think of regimental reunions).
- We are most likely to be influenced by those whose beliefs are strangest to us. This is simply because we have usually given the matters concerned little or no thought. We have no 'defences' against the strange argument. By this reasoning, people caught up in 'political terrorism' hostage-takings may be most likely of all to have their attitudes changed. The 1985 hijacking in Beirut of a TWA Boeing 727 provides a good example of this. The event was particularly fruitful for the hi-jackers (who murdered one hostage) because many of the hostages returned to the USA as virtual propagandists for their captors. Because the hostages had not thought much about the politics of the Middle East before their ordeal, most were quite easily persuaded of the terrorists' point of view.

This type of susceptibility is related to what is known in psychology as an attitude-inoculation effect. Giving people some practice at discussing and refuting arguments is necessary for them to be able to withstand major influence attempts. Of course the effect is also relevant in circumstances like the conversion of young people to fringe religions. The case of the heiress Patti Hearst should be mentioned here. She joined the organization which captured her. Since her life had been a fairly restricted one in many ways, she is precisely the sort of person one could predict would be subject to the Stockholm syndrome.

While the Stockholm syndrome is an interesting curiosity in psychological terms, it should not be over-emphasized. It is not an inevitable occurrence. A recent study found it to have occurred in only one of seven hostages. While it cannot be relied upon, the Stockholm syndrome can be a useful ally. If someone is fond of you, you tend to be fond of them. If a hostage becomes fond of the captor, all but the most hardened of hostage takers will find it more difficult to harm the hostage. Of course, the Stockholm syndrome can also work against the negotiator — It turned Patti Hearst into a machine-gun-toting bank robber — and can lead to bizarre situations where the captor gives the hostage a gun to hold while he eats – and gets it back!

It has been suggested that the people who suffer least as hostages are those who:

- had good physical health prior to capture
- had a rich and satisfying life before capture
- had a strong self-identity
- had a clear sense of purpose and meaning in their lives
- had a sense of objectives for which to live
- had a record of success and achievement in life.

Once captured, hostages go through a number of stages during their captivity. The usual order is as follows:

- a sense of isolation
- a search for meaning in the situation
- taking stock of the elements in the situation
- organizing and attempting to assess some sort of control over the hostile environment
- planning, establishing goals and future directions for life.

These stages can obviously take place alongside a developing relationship with the captor. They also bear a substantial resemblance to the stages which are normally identified as following bereavement or some other major loss or life change (see Chapter 9). In a sense there are similarities. You can grieve for your lost freedom and adjust to your new situation, and you may anticipate the ultimate bereavement, that of yourself! The stages of bereavement are also similar to those which people who know that they are dying go through.

Coming to terms with freedom

While there is an obvious temptation to dwell on the more dramatic events of hostage taking itself, it would be wise to pay a little attention to the problems which may follow release. As we note in Chapter 12, it is not only unpleasant events which cause stress. Stress can be a component of any major change in circumstances. Very lengthy debriefing of released hostages is now the order of the day. People must come to terms with their freedom and with the way in which they are to regard themselves after release. Hallucinations are one of the documented effects of the release. A more insidious one may have been guessed at by any readers who have made linkages between Chapter 7 and this one.

In Chapter 7 we discussed the fundamental attribution error. An example of this well-established principle is that people in impossible situations are to an unreasonable degree blamed for what has happened to them. Released hostages will to a certain extent be regarded as responsible for their own capture, responsible for not overpowering their captors, responsible for not making determined escape attempts. If the former hostage is in fact subject to the Stockholm syndrome too (like the stewardess held at pistol point who continued to bring her hijacker gifts in prison long after his arrest) then the obvious conclusion which other people will reach is that the hostage was responsible or was colluding with the hijacker.

This is a difficult problem. The questions really start getting asked about the heiress Patti Hearst, who helped her captors, the Symbionese Liberation Army, to hold up a bank. Miss Hearst showed the Stockholm syndrome in large measure, and came from a background where she had never experienced the kind of political view expressed by the Symbionese Liberation Army and so was easily swayed by them. Interestingly, Miss Hearst went on to show a kind of reverse Stockholm syndrome, falling in love with and marrying one of the police officers involved in her release. No doubt the police culture with which she was equally unfamiliar was also conducive to swift attitude change!

Patti Hearst has money and social status to cushion the effects of her problems. However, even the rich and secure are not exempt from the fundamental attribution error. Her real sentence is that the situation drove her to do what she did. Paradoxically, having an expensive lawyer to argue the point on her behalf makes ordinary people even less likely to believe her. To a lesser extent, the same life sentence faces all former hostages.

Review notes

The skills needed in hostage situations are primarily communication skills. Detailed information about the hostage-taker, while important, is less critical than skilled negotiation.

In hostage situations, surprisingly small concessions can produce an end to the seige. Delay gives more chance for the captor to see hostages as real people, and be less inclined towards harm.

Some hostages develop warm relationships with their captors. This may seem strange in cases where the ideology of the hostage-taker is alien to the victim. However it is in these circumstances that the development of bonds of friendship or affection may be most likely to develop.

Many hostages have particular difficulty in re-adjusting to freedom.

References

McKenzie, I.K. (1981) Hostage–captor relationships. *Bulletin of The British Psychological Society, 34,* 161–163.
Miron, M.S. and Goldstein, A.P. (1979) *Hostage.* Oxford: Pergamon.
Siegel, R.K. (1984) Hostage hallucinations: Visual imagery induced by isolation and life-threatening stress. *Journal of Nervous and Mental Disease, 172,* 264–272.

Further reading

McKenzie, I.K. (1981) Hostage–captor relationships. *Bulletin of The British Psychological Society, 34,* 161–163.
McKenzie, I.K. (1985) The siege mentality. *Police Review,* 26 April, 848-849.
Miron, M.S. and Goldstein, A.P. (1979) *Hostage.* Oxford: Pergamon.

Chapter 11

Criminals

You may well be starting this chapter with an inclination to be sceptical. You may anticipate an outpouring of sentimentality from two bleeding-heart psychologists, with criminality blamed on deprived childhoods and the lack of mother figures. You will get a little of that, plus a good deal more that you probably do not expect. The chapter is in two parts. The first is a fairly straightforward account of some of the ways in which psychology has addressed the problem of criminality. In the second, we take a step back and try to assess whether psychology has anything to say which may help police officers in making practical judgements about offenders. We do this using the important example of the decision whether to caution or to send offenders forward for prosecution.

Born criminals

The oldest form of psychological tradition is one which links criminal behaviour with inherited characteristics. In Italy in the last century Cesare Lombroso claimed to have found a 'criminal type'. Some of the signs he detected were receding foreheads, relative insensitivity to pain, lobeless ears and distinctive creasing of the palm. Lombroso saw this criminal type as a primitive form of human being. The skull of the brigand Vilella (the study of which led Lombroso to his theory) is now displayed in the Criminological Museum in Rome.

The idea of a criminal type also crops up in the work of those who have sought to link criminal behaviour with body build. The basic idea is that a person's genetic blueprint (genotype) includes plans for both mental and physical attributes, and that in this blueprint certain kinds of body build and personality type go together in the same way that certain eye colours tend to go with certain hair colours. Theorists of this point of view have tended to associate muscular body types with the tendency to commit crime.

It is easy now to ridicule early 'criminal type' theories. It seems nowadays that Cesare Lombroso is mentioned in books only to be laughed at for his florid language and his extravagant claims. Yet Lombroso and other 'criminal type' theorists were great men advancing a young discipline. What is clear is that their theories were much too simple. For instance, the observations Lombroso made were of people in institutions which contained many who were severely mentally impaired and who may well for that reason have shown some of the signs that Lombroso took to be marks of criminality. Any link between body build and criminality is much more readily explained by the likelihood that muscular people are sought after as allies in crime, because they can succeed where their weedier companions would fail.

Whilst we may now quite safely discount many early 'criminal type' theories, more recent research requires more careful attention. One of the reasons why Lombroso's theory was accepted was that society had a need to 'make sense of' behaviour which was otherwise difficult to explain. It was comforting for people to be told that criminals were different from the rest of us law-abiding citizens, and were, literally, a breed apart. By accepting this theory people could take comfort in the fact that no matter what the circumstances, they would never commit a crime! Whenever a notorious villain is apprehended (the Yorkshire Ripper is an example which springs immediately to mind) people try to understand how they could have done what they did. How much easier people feel when they have been able to label the person as different from the rest of us.

Let us look now at the modern theory of 'criminal type', the XYY syndrome. Biologists have established that we are born with certain characteristics which are contained within 23 pairs of chromosomes. Certain abnormalities in human behaviour can be traced directly to genetic abnormalities in the chromosomes. The best known example is Down's syndrome (formerly known as mongolism), which is a condition caused entirely by the possession of an extra chromosome on the 21st pair. This genetic defect has an effect on the physical and mental condition of anyone affected. Other abnormalities in our genetic make-up may also have an effect. For example, one pair of chromosomes determines whether we are born male (XY) or female (XX). However, some men are born with an extra male chromosome, thereby being labelled XYY or 'supermale'. We will now consider this as a modern example of a biological crime theory.

Men of all ages acquire more criminal convictions than do women. In England and Wales a man aged 28 is nearly *five times* as likely to have been convicted of a non-trivial offence as a woman of 28. It is not surprising, then, that people with an extra Y chromosome would be thought to have criminal tendencies. Although the first man ever found to possess an extra Y was perfectly law-abiding, surveys in secure hospitals and prisons did show that there were more people there with an extra Y chromosome than you would expect (given their rate in the general population). Some gruesome murders committed by men with an extra Y chromosome did nothing at all for their image! There were voices raised suggesting that men found to have an extra Y chromosome should be detained as a preventive measure, *before* they had done anything bad. One description applied to them was 'walking powder kegs'. Some multiple murderers who did not have an extra Y chromosome were rumoured to have it. A television series was named 'The XYY Man' after the syndrome, perhaps to reflect the ruthlessness of its 'hero'.

To cut a long and interesting story short, it was found that there had been an error in the estimation of the number of men with the extra Y chromosome in the population generally. There were a lot more of them roaming about than was originally thought. That meant that their numbers in secure hospitals and prisons was not so remarkably high, in proportion to their number outside. It was also found that XYY detainees had committed *less* serious offences than detainees without the extra chromosome. While there is an association of the extra Y chromosome and criminality, the best guess is that this is because of the mild mental impairment frequent in men with an extra Y chromosome – and low intelligence *is* associated with higher rates of criminality. In other words, it is likely that you find extra Y men over-represented in prisons because they are on average less intelligent, not because the extra chromosome turns them into monsters.

What is the moral of this story? It is that people rushed, prematurely, to fall in behind a view of criminality which implied 'bad seed'. It is convenient for the public to see criminals as monsters, nothing like the ordinary citizen, and basically bad. The extra Y chromosome encouraged this view of criminality, and it was seized upon with indecent haste. It should teach us to be more cautious in our enthusiasm for biologically based theories of criminal type. There is some recent and perfectly respectable research suggesting that there might be a slight tendency for criminality to run in families. In such research, the children of criminal parents who are adopted are compared with the children of non-criminal parents who go for adoption. However, we are talking about, at most, a slightly higher risk of developing a criminal record. The data fall very far short of the idea that the children of convicted offenders have a 'mark of Cain' which leads them irresistibly into crime.

Psychological theories stressing the environment

If you asked a police officer or member of the public to describe a psychological theory of crime, he or she would almost certainly come up with some version of a theory of environmental deprivation, featuring broken homes, school failure and unemployment. The theory is perhaps most succinctly stated in a song from the musical *West Side Story*. The weary police officer is told by gang members 'I'm depraved on account of I'm deprived'.

The founder of psychoanalysis, Sigmund Freud, saw conscience as originating in the relations between parents and families, with delinquent behaviour a sign of faulty development. The best-known extension of this theory comes from John Bowlby in the late 1940s and early 1950s. He suggested that neurotic delinquency or criminality can be the result of 'maternal deprivation'. This somewhat woolly term includes the physical separation of mother and child. It also includes mother–child relationships which are continuous but disturbed. What many people have since objected to in Bowlby's theory is the suggestion that distorted relationships in early childhood create *permanent* damage, and that there is something mystical in the mother–child relationship. Later evidence suggests that damage caused by absent or distorted parent–child relationships *can* be repaired by good links with adults later in childhood. Also, it is no longer thought that there is anything particular about the mother beyond the fact that she has traditionally been the parent who does more parenting. There has been a reaction against the central position assigned to the mother, and much psychological work during the 1960s and 70s focused on the father. Psychologists now think of the whole social context of child-rearing rather than one which focuses on one or other parent. We develop this theme presently.

For the moment, we would like to describe one important piece of research evidence with practical implications. It has been found that loving homes with a single parent produce *lower* rates of delinquency than intact families with conflict in the home. It is important to stress that broken homes by themselves do not spawn delinquents. It is the conflict in the home that is more crucial than its composition.

One tradition in *sociological* theories of crime must be included here. This is the idea that simply getting tangled up in the criminal justice system is a bad thing. The stigma of a criminal conviction (either your own or a member of the family's) or living in a particular area may change the way you see yourself. It may also lead you to commit more crime. It may, by alerting the police, make you more likely to be convicted after committing a criminal act. There is some evidence for this from a number of research studies and it is important for one obvious reason. Given that the peak age of known offending is in the mid to late teens (after which a lot of people give up crime), it seems a good strategy to try to do as little as possible to offenders until they really get to be career criminals. Most adolescents commit some crime, after all. This idea lies behind cautioning. It is much strengthened by the evidence that getting involved in the system actually increases your chances of offending again.

The most important contribution to understanding the development of delinquency over the last 20 years has been the large-scale research of Donald West and David Farrington, known as the 'Cambridge longitudinal study'. It involved following up some 400 London boys from the age of 8 to 25. It has proved possible to establish those factors which distinguished boys who went on to pick up a criminal record from those who did not. As Donald West (1982) notes:

> Theorists, both sociological and psychological, have sometimes tended to place emphasis on one particular event or circumstance. A broken home, lack of parental affection, insufficient discipline, poverty and neighbourhood culture have each in turn been credited with being the main cause of delinquency. Our study, because it encompassed a wide range of items, was able to show that delinquency most often arises from an accumulation of different pressures rather than from any single salient cause.

The Cambridge study identified five key factors affecting the likelihood of becoming delinquent. These were:

- coming from a low-income family
- coming from a large (5 +) family
- having parents considered by social workers to have performed

their child-rearing duties unsatisfactorily
- having well below average intelligence (IQ score of less than 90)
- having a parent with a criminal record acquired before the child's tenth birthday.

Of the boys who had a combination of at least three of the predictive factors, almost one half became delinquent, as compared with only a fifth among the sample as a whole.

Another approach to the same sort of issue comes from the work of Al Blumstein and his colleagues. They thought that the important thing was to be able to predict the number of juveniles who will become chronic (that is persistent) offenders and the number who will desist from crime. Using data from the Cambridge study, they found seven childhood factors which distinguished chronic from non-chronic offenders. The numbers in brackets refer to the age at which the relevant measurement took place. The factors were:

convicted early (10–13)
low family income (8)
teacher rating of troublesomeness at school (8–10)
poor school attainment (8–10)
clumsiness (8–10)
low non-verbal intelligence (8–10)
convicted brother or sister (10).

The factors identified by West and by Blumstein are important. However, West himself, certainly the most experienced researcher in British delinquency, sees them as only part of the picture. West was trained as a psychiatrist and may be regarded as likely to overstate the effects of personal rather than environmental factors. Despite this, in his diagram, on page 134, illustrating some of the possible major influences on delinquency (Figure 11.1) you can see the variety of factors which affect delinquency.

Are crime and criminality useful ideas?

So far we have talked about crime as if it were like big feet or blue eyes – that it is a real, out in the world characteristic of people. You only need a ruler to work out whether people have big feet or not. But what about crime? The only thing that fraud, mugging and soliciting have in common is that parliament has decided that they are serious enough to do something about. In the same way, lumping together *people* who commit these kinds of offences seems strange. Certainly for the purposes of preventing *crime*, lumping

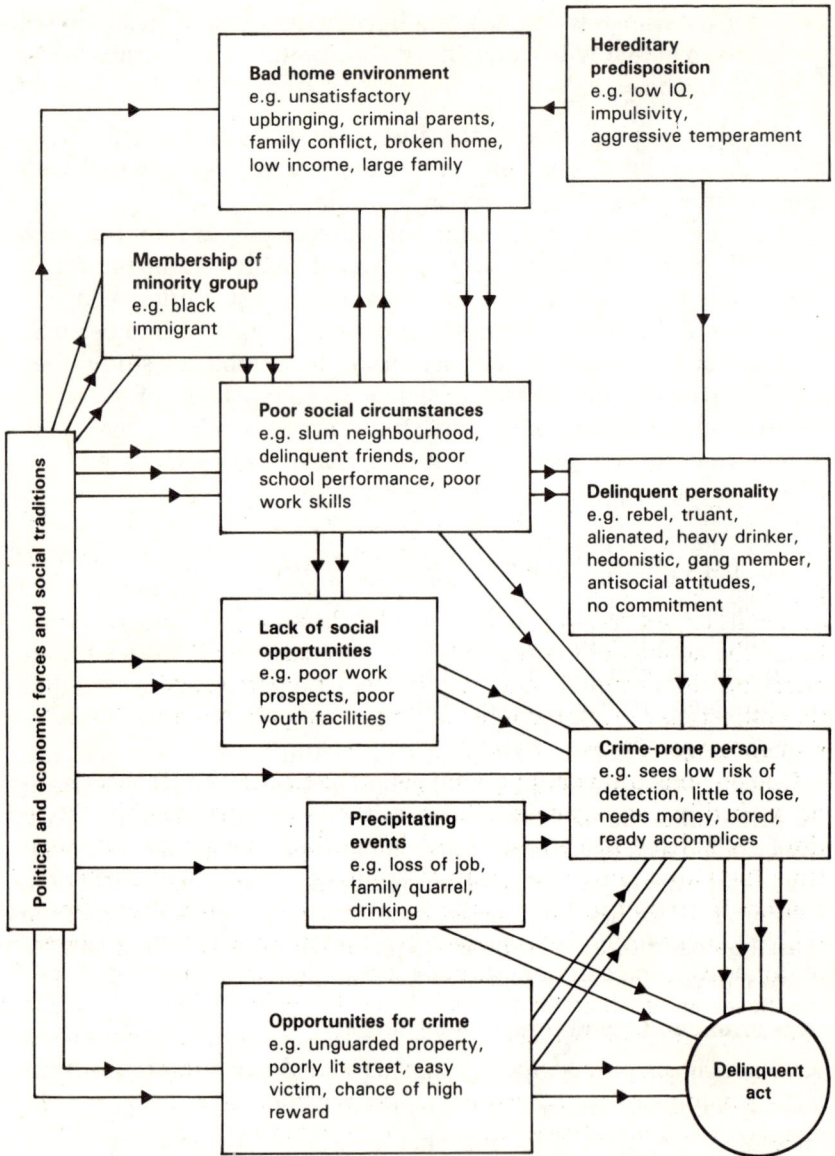

Figure 11.1. Major influences contributing to delinquent behaviour.

From D.J. West (1982) *Delinquency: Its Roots, Careers and Prospects.* Reprinted with the permission of the publishers, Gower Publishing Company Limited.

events together is strange. For crime prevention it is important to be absolutely detailed and specific about what you are doing and how it might prevent crime. Leaving a bedroom light on when you go out might stop your house being burgled but it is quite irrelevant to your chances of being mugged. It is as well to remember this, rather than obscuring it by combining both events as crimes. However, for reasons which are common sense if you think about them, what to do about crime is a different problem from what to do about criminals. Many serious crimes remain uncleared. A large majority of those convicted are first-timers in the dock, and a majority of first-time offenders are not convicted again.

Does it make sense to talk about *criminals* rather than burglars and vandals and rapists? We would argue that for some purposes the more general term is useful. An important and consistent research finding is that it is the *minority* of repeat criminals who *specialize* in a particular offence.

Table 11.1. Males born in 1953, 1958 and 1963 and convicted of one or more standard list offences before the age of 16, by principal type of offence on first conviction, and reconviction outcome after two years

Principal offence on first conviction	Percentage reconvicted of offence of same type	Percentage reconvicted of different offence	Percentage not reconvicted
Violence against the person	2	28	69*
Burglary (incl. robbery)	19	25	57
Theft and handling stolen goods	16	20	64
Fraud and forgery	0	38	63
Criminal damage	3	24	73
Other indictable offences	2	34	64
Summary offences (excl. motoring)	3	25	72
Motoring (mainly theft/ unauthorized taking)	9	30	60
Total	16 195	57 005	73 200

*Note Rows do not always sum to precisely 100 because of rounding

From K. Pease, What risk reconviction of juveniles? *Justice of the Peace*, 149, 329. Reprinted with the permission of the proprietors, Justice of the Peace Ltd.

Table 11.1 shows the probability of reconviction of juveniles *by type of offence*. It is evident that no group specializes to the extent that the second conviction is more likely than not to be for the same type of offence as the first. Most criminal careers are *diverse*. This suggests that it does make some sort of sense to talk about criminals in a general way, even though the acts which are thereby lumped together are so various. But we should not overstate the case: few armed robbers turn to cheque fraud. To summarize, we are arguing that it is not sensible to deal with crime as a whole when the purpose is crime prevention. When, on the other hand, the purpose is dealing with detected offenders, there is something to be said for treating criminality as a single general category, because offenders are versatile.

For a police officer, there is a strict limit to how useful psychological theories of crime are in his or her work. The police officer cannot change the genetic make-up of people or revolutionize the nation's child-rearing practices. However, there is a relevance, which we expand on in the next section.

Police theories of criminality

Every time a police officer decides whether or not to caution an offender, underpinning that action is a personal theory of crime. Every time the police react adversely (or favourably, but that seems less common) to the pronouncement of a sentence, they do so on the basis of a personal theory of crime as it applies to the person in the dock. So while you may not feel any enthusiasm for theories of crime (or indeed for any sort of theory), you have got your own, whether you are aware of them or not, and they colour your policing decisions. These beliefs may inform decisions about women offenders, for example. There is an argument (hotly contested by feminists) that women get preferential treatment from male police officers. Beliefs about whether serious motoring offences can be regarded as 'real crime' also influence decisions made. We have chosen to illustrate the issue by reference to decisions made about juvenile offenders.

Most juvenile first offenders are dealt with by cautioning. The decision to take no action, to caution or to proceed, is perhaps the most obvious one where a personal theory of crime comes into play. The evidence reviewed earlier that a conviction itself increases the likelihood of further offending is a powerful argument for being as sparing as possible with the court process. Let us give an example of one force's cautioning practice, and try to deduce the police theory of crime underpinning it. We thereupon enter the murky area between psychology and justice.

Figure 11.2 describes one force's cautioning *practice*. It is important to emphasize that the data come from a single force because even the most recent guidelines on cautioning are terribly woolly. Psychological research has shown many strange things, but none stranger than the fact that people can be behaving perfectly systematically in terms of one theory, while justifying their actions in terms of a totally different one. Figure 11.2 shows those factors which are associated most closely with decisions to caution. You will see in the top box of the figure the rate of cautioning in the sample studied. It shows that 62.2 per cent of the sample was cautioned. The sample is then broken down by the factor which is the best single predictor of the cautioning decision. In other words, if you had to guess whether someone was cautioned, and were only allowed one question before you made your guess, the question you should ask is about offender age. Younger children were cautioned more often (86.9 per cent) than their elders (30.4 per cent). Concentrating now on the younger children only, the next important factor is whether they say they are sorry. If they did, they were very likely (94.8 per cent) to get cautioned. If they did not they were much less likely to get cautioned (59.1 per cent). If they were young and said they were sorry, and it was their first offence, that virtually clinched it. If they were not sorry, the next important factor was whether they came from a good home. If they were not sorry but came from a good home, they were much more likely to be cautioned than if they were not sorry but came from a bad home. In this way, it looks as though the quality of the child's home is a sort of substitute for the child himself being sorry. Having now gone down the whole of the left-hand side of Figure 11.2 in some detail, you will be able to interpret the right-hand side for yourself. Clearly the nature of the offence is much more important for children of 14-plus as far as the police officer is concerned. Being sorry, you will note, does not help significantly if the offence is shoplifting!

Figure 11.2 incorporates a theory of criminality. It is one in which youth and remorse are judged by the police to be good signs for giving up crime. If you are older, the type of crime committed is judged central in deciding likely development of a criminal career. We are in no way suggesting that this is a general police theory, just that it shapes action in at least one force. Let us now think about this. Why are younger children cautioned more often? Early onset of criminal career is an indicator of more criminality in the long run. Why should those more likely to continue in crime be favoured in comparison with other people? Why should coming from a good home make you more likely to be cautioned – is it not enough that someone is socially disadvantaged, without prosecuting him or her as well? If you are observant you will notice that these two questions lead in opposite directons. The first implies that cautioning should be based on a prediction of what is likely to happen in the future. The second implies that cautioning should be based on blame, that is, on what has been done, purely and simply.

The tension between blame and prediction is a feature of the whole criminal justice process, from cautioning to parole. For example, do you parole those who have been model prisoners but whose background suggests they will offend on release? What happens if the prisoner's spouse is having affairs during the enforced separation? You cannot blame the prisoner for that, but you can realistically predict trouble upon release. Do you release someone whose offence and background suggest a low probability of reconviction but who keeps assaulting fellow prisoners? Unfortunately there is no right answer to these questions. It depends on your personal values, and on your view of the penal system. Basically it depends on what you think is fair and what you think is unfair. Your decision about what is fair should, properly, precede your decision about how you will use the psychological theories in this chapter.

Let us now stand back and review the course of this chapter so far. We have described some of the major strands in psychological thought concerning the development of criminality. We have been sceptical of biological theories of crime, and of the cruder environmental theories. We have argued that the work of Donald West and David Farrington provides the best available basis for understanding juvenile crime. The work of Al Blumstein and his colleagues also provides evidence about the people who will persist in crime. Yet just because you have the ability to predict does not mean that you will decide that it is fair to do so. Just because psychologists provide some relevant facts does not mean you should *unthinkingly* apply them. Cautioning practice is once again the obvious example. If you caution those who, on West's guidelines, are less likely to be reconvicted, the other side of the coin is that you are advocating less lenient treatment for children who are already socially and personally disadvantaged. It is a real problem, and officers will be pressured to caution those from good homes in good areas who say they are sorry. 'We'll take care of this, officer, you can rest assured

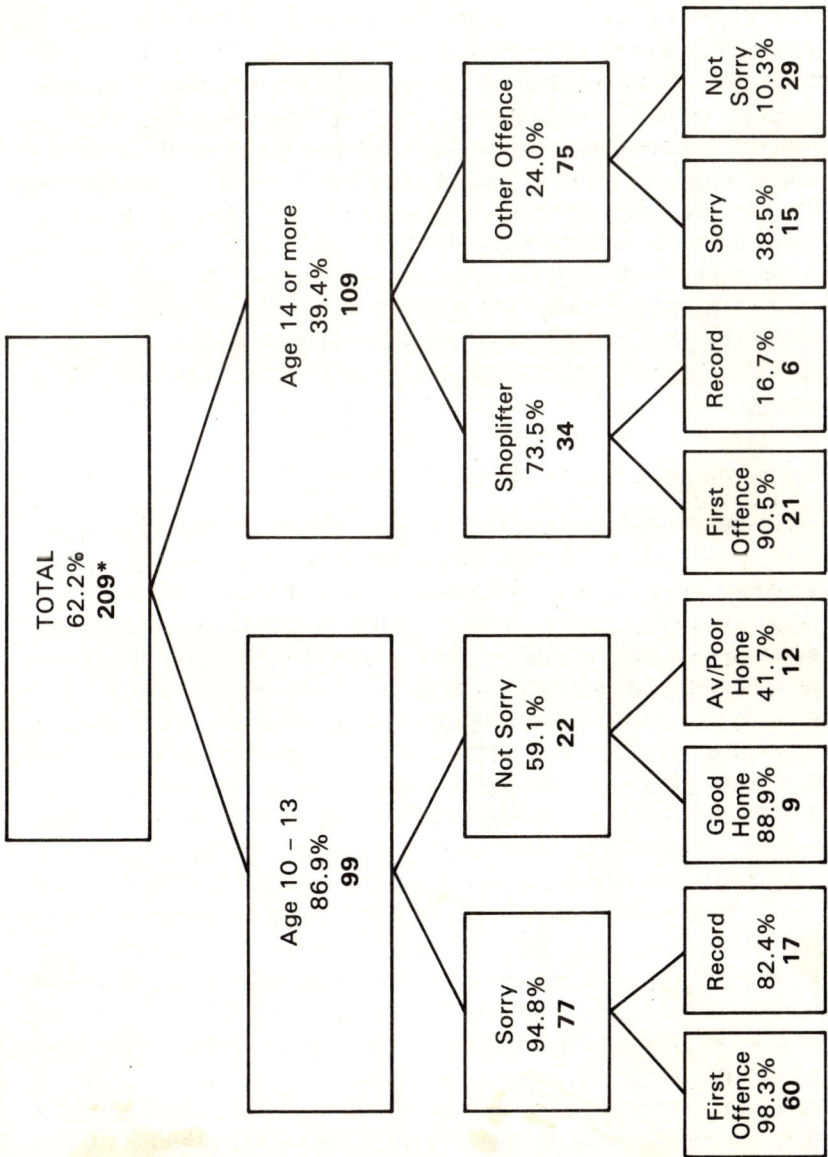

* In each case number in bold refers to total who were either cautioned or prosecuted.

Figure 11.2. For those for whom the outcome is known, percentages in different categories who were cautioned rather than prosecuted.

it won't happen again ... He's going to a child guidance clinic now and it's making a big difference ... You can see he comes from a good home, please don't ruin it' and so on.

One constructive move is to increase the amount of cautioning generally. Table 11.1 shows that the odds are the convicted juveniles will *not* be reconvicted within two years. On the evidence, cautioning would be no less effective than conviction in reducing further convictions. There is thus scope for one extra caution for all juvenile offenders. We would still end up with reconvictions for less than half of those cautioned for the extra time. In this way, the extra cautioning generally would reduce the impact of the system on those already socially disadvantaged and thus reduce the *relative* disadvantage. It will not however reduce the absolute level of disadvantage.

Postscript: is there psychology after sentence?

We have concentrated on the early stages in the criminal justice system, as we believe that will be of most interest to police officers. However, psychological theory and practice is relevant after conviction. Alcoholics may find themselves convicted of offences committed while in drink, people who find it difficult to keep their temper may find themselves convicted of offences of violence, crime victims may suffer severe anxiety, and so on. There is a prison psychological service, but it is small and therefore cannot easily deliver treatment services to prisoners. What is more, to quote one prison psychologist 'We are prison psychologists, not prisoner psychologists'. In other words, there are lots of aspects of prison life to which psychological skills are relevant. One of them of course is the fact that prisons do change the ways of thinking of people living or working in them (see Chapter 7).

Outside prisons there are clinical and educational psychologists whose services are available to offenders and victims of crime, as well as to other members of the public. Probation and supervision orders obviously involve counselling offenders, and psychiatric treatment is one of the conditions which may be attached to a probation order. Orders under mental health legislation have declined in number, but are still available for offenders whose conditions are judged to be treatable. This has led to a dramatic decline in the number of mentally impaired people being sentenced under this legislation. Some psychologists think that a life crisis produces a willingness in people to change their lives, and so the crisis is also a chance to change. This does not mean that offenders should get harsher sentences *so that* they can be treated, although this is a pressure to which sentencers often succumb, notably with the introduction of youth custody in place of Borstal training. After that change, sentencers were clearly giving longer sentences than before so that young offenders could go to institutions which clearly offered training rather than ones which did not. The principle enunciated by Norval Morris needs reading twice but is sound. It is that sentencing should never be harsher than it would be if reform were not one of its purposes.

Review notes

Biological theories of crime are in disrepute, although there may well be genetic predisposing factors in crime. Social factors including low income, poor parenting, low IQ and early criminal involvement do predispose towards persistent criminality. Criminal careers are usually varied, with the specialist in a single type of crime being less common that the generalist.

The transient nature of most juvenile crime is an important point to recognize. The best prediction is that a juvenile offender on first conviction will not be convicted again within two years.

Police practice *always* contains an implicit theory of criminal development. Sometimes this theory means that people are treated unfairly, by being dealt with according to the officer's implicit theory of crime.

Some psychological treatment is available and may be helpful for some offenders after conviction.

References

Blumstein, A., Farrington, D.P. and Moitra, S. (1985) Delinquency careers: Innocents, desisters and persisters. In M. Tonry and N. Morris (eds) *Crime and Justice 6.* Chicago: University of Chicago Press.
Fisher, C.J. and Mawby, R.I. (1982) Juvenile delinquency and police discretion in an inner-city area. *British Journal of Criminlogy, 22,* 63–75.
Pease, K. (1983) What risk of reconviction for juveniles? *Justice of the Peace, 149,* 329.
Walker, N. (1980) *Punishment, Danger and Stigma.* Oxford: Basil Blackwell.
West, D.J. (1982) *Delinquency: Its Roots, Careers and Prospects.* London: Heinemann.

Further reading

Feldman, M.P. (1977) *Criminal Behaviour*. Chichester: Wiley.
West, D.J. (1982) *Delinquency: Its Roots, Careers and Prospects*. London: Heinemann.

Chapter 12

Stress and the Police Officer

The Sunday Times of 3 February 1985 ran a story under the headline 'Police demand special aid to combat stress'. The Police Federation had engaged in a period of active lobbying for attention to be paid to the problems of stress in police work. The Federation held a symposium concerned with stress in October 1984. Canadian research suggests that disorders with psychosomatic components (headaches, indigestion, constipation, diarrhoea, high blood pressure and ulcers) are more frequent among police officers than among citizens generally.

The problem made headlines in Great Britain early in 1985. An inspector with a provincial force was its central and tragic figure. He had a long and unblemished career. He appears to have been driven beyond endurance by problems centring on a gipsy encampment. He took a gun and shot up the camp (without injuring anyone). His solicitor blamed 'the stress of police work' for making his client ill at the time of the shooting. 'He held down a demanding job with considerable responsibilities. His wife was also ill, and he had to try to look after her at the same time.'

We fear that some of his colleagues may have been less charitable. 'He lost his bottle' comes to mind as the likely reaction from his less sympathetic colleagues. All in all stress is an 'in' word (and its cousin, 'professional burn-out' will be even more in vogue by the time this book is published). It reflects real problems, but it is one of those elusive words, like 'community' and 'professional'. When you try to put your finger on the exact meaning, it squirts out from underneath like a sliver of wet soap.

Is stress something that is *imposed* on you (a stimulus) or is it a way in which you *react* to the world (a response)? Common language would lead you to think of it as a stimulus. People are described as being 'under stress'. The unhappy inspector just discussed was described as suffering from 'the stress of police work', implying that that is where it came from. The only trouble with thinking of stress as 'something that happens to you' is the enormous range of different responses to the same, overtly nasty situation. In World War I, some soldiers doggedly went 'over the top' of their trenches to likely death time after time. In contrast, some forgot who they were and what they were doing and simply wandered away, suffering from 'shell-shock'. Some bus drivers retire in good health, others, driving the same routes, get stomach ulcers or heart attacks. Thinking of stress simply as a stimulus cannot account for this variety of response.

On the other hand, thinking of stress purely as a response ignores the fact that some events, like the death or illness of a loved one, make most of us behave in unusual ways. So we have to think of stress from two different perspectives. It may be helpful to think of stress in the engineering sense. A material is said to be stressed when a force has been applied to it, but the word also refers to the changes produced in the material. We have to think of the stress potential of different situations and also the changes produced in people.

People vary greatly in the nature of the situations they find stressful, the extremity of the situations needed to evoke a stress response, and how the stressed response will manifest itself. This suggests three ways in which psychology might aid an understanding of stress:

- Identification of ways in which changing some aspect of a situation can serve to make it less stressful.
- Identification of situations with general and inevitable high stress potential, so that when people are placed in them, they are properly trained and supported.
- Suggestion of ways in which individuals might be helped to overcome the worst of their stress reactions.

We should pause at this point to state that we would not like you to think that the total absence of stress is a good thing, and that any stress is a bad thing. The only state which is completely stress-free is death. People perform best under a modicum of stress, with more complex jobs having a lower optimum stress level. In this chapter, however, we deal primarily with the common situation in which stress is above the optimum level, so that its effect is to harm performance.

The stress potential of situations

A good place to start is a list of which situations have the greatest stress potential for people in general. Discussion of this is included here for two reasons. First because it gives a rough idea of the kinds of life events you personally may regard as stressful, and second because it may help give insight into the responses of those with whom you have to deal in the course of your job.

T.H. Holmes and R.H. Rahe (1967) were the researchers who pioneered the *Social readjustment rating scale*, which is reproduced in simplified form as Table 12.1. The underlying idea is that stress affects susceptibility to illness. This is reasonably well established and probably accords with your own experience. First you get run down by work or family problems, and then the virus takes over. So Holmes and Rahe found out those life events which preceded the onset of illness. They then calculated the closeness of the relationship between the event and the illness, and gave the event a stress score in accordance with that – so that the more predictably an event precedes an illness, the more stressful it is judged to be, and the higher the stress score it is assigned.

So, in Table 12.1, the most stressful event is death of a spouse. Being sacked is quite stressing, and a change in social activities is slightly stressing. Adding up the items which apply to you gives a total score, a 'life crisis unit'. The higher the score the greater the likelihood of developing an illness. You might be surprised to find in the list some happy-looking items. Yet marriage, marital reconciliation and Christmas are all in the list as having stress potential. If we have got the right idea of the main readership of this book, you may have just embarked on marriage, or be just about to. If so, you probably need little telling about the stress potential of the happy day. In fact *any* change (promotion as well as demotion, gain as well as loss of family members) has been found to be linked with susceptibility to disease. When lives are in a steady state, less illness is suffered. This fact should be linked to the approach you might like to take when intervening in crises, so it would help for you to make links between this chapter and Chapter 9.

Let us remind you of an important qualification. Just because you can grade the stress potential of events, it does not mean that all people who encounter them feel stressed. To be cynical, the death of a rich old wife might be just what a grabbing young husband wants. Even the death of a much-loved wife may not be a stressor. It depends on how the widower sees it. If he is religious, or if he sees

Table 12.1. The social readjustment rating scale

Life event	Mean value
1. Death of spouse	100
2. Divorce	73
3. Marital separation	65
4. Jail term	63
5. Death of close family member	63
6. Personal injury or illness	53
7. Marriage	50
8. Fired at work	47
9. Marital reconciliation	45
10. Retirement	45
11. Change in health of family member	44
12. Pregnancy	40
13. Sex difficulties	39
14. Gain of new family member	39
15. Business readjustment	39
16. Change in financial state	38
17. Death of close friend	37
18. Change to different line of work	36
19. Change in number of arguments with spouse	35
20. Mortgage over $10,000	31
21. Foreclosure of mortgage or loan	30
22. Change in responsibilities at work	29
23. Son or daughter leaving home	29
24. Trouble with in-laws	29
25. Outstanding personal achievement	28
26. Wife begin or stop work	26
27. Begin or end school	26
28. Change in living conditions	25
29. Revision of personal habits	24
30. Trouble with boss	23
31. Change in work hours or conditions	20
32. Change in residence	20
33. Change in schools	20
34. Change in recreation	19
35. Change in church activities	19
36. Change in social activities	18
37. Mortgage or loan less than $10,000	17
38. Change in sleeping habits	16
39. Change in number of family get-togethers	15
40. Change in eating habits	15
41. Vacation	13
42. Christmas	12
43. Minor violations of the law	11

Adapted from T.H. Holmes and R.H. Rahe 'The social readjustment rating scale', *Journal of Psychosomatic Research*, 11, 213–218. Reprinted with the permission of the publishers, Pergamon Press.

the death as a release from pain, the reaction will be different. The second qualification is this: even if the event does evoke a stressed response, that response does not have to be illness. It is just that illness was a convenient basis for Holmes and Rahe in the development of their scale. To continue with our example, the response to a spouse's death could be illness or a range of other reactions, up to and including hallucinations of the dead person. You may be shocked to find that some kind and sympathetic people respond to both bad and good news with hysterical laughter. One of the requirements for police officers before they can help skillfully is the recognition that such unusual reactions will take place. Hysterical laughter is not callousness and the hallucinations of the bereaved are probably not symptoms of mental illness.

So much for situations likely to evoke stress in people in general. How about stress in the police officer in particular? There is no thorough and well-grounded work on police officers which is comparable with the Holmes and Rahe work, but there is a very useful British first shot which is based on simply asking 93 officers at Bramshill Police College about the stress potential of 45 states or situations which police officers might face. The scale, which is comparable in form to the Holmes and Rahe scale, is reproduced here as Table 12.2. It has a number of very interesting features. At the most stressful end of the scale there are found a set of, thankfully infrequent, dramatic stressors centring on terrorists and weapons. The second group (leaving aside for the moment the interesting 'Having to do things against your moral principles', to which we return) are to do with relationships among officers, like 'Having to cover up for a colleague' and 'Being caught making a mistake'. These were identified as more stressful than 'Seeing mutilated bodies' and 'Having to deal with a messy car accident'. The exercise of and submission to authority were the subject of remarkably little stress.

Despite the relatively low rating of 'Seeing mutilated bodies', we cannot assume that the most extreme horrors will leave people unaffected. One example, from Liam McAuley (1981), will suffice:

A young officer ran into a burning house and rescued two children but was forced to stand helplessly by as two others died screaming. He received an award for bravery. But it was months before he could admit to having recurring nightmares of children screaming and then no help was given by his department. Rather, he was admitted to a mental hospital and as a direct result was retired from the police service on medical grounds.

Warren Young tells us of the severe psychological effects suffered by policemen who had to clear the human debris of the Air New Zealand DC10 crash in Antarctica.

Returning to the Bramshill scale, it is interesting rather than conclusive. The scale is based on what *senior* officers *thought* would be stressful, rather than what was really stressful as measured by, for example, how often you become ill afterwards. There are no pleasant events in the list at all, and there should be. Holmes and Rahe showed they could be substantially stressful. It would have been interesting to see whether the senior officers concerned would have marked events like promotion as stressful. Nonetheless there is support for the other main strand of Holmes and Rahe's theory, namely that change events are the stressful ones. Items near the top of Table 12.2 *tend* to be associated with change events of uncertain outcome and, interestingly, where the officer is helpless to determine the way things turn out. In other words, unpredictable and uncontrollable outcomes cause stress. Whether you see yourself as having *control* over events is an important element in stress responses, and we return to this point later.

Four weeks after the report of the Bramshill research appeared in *Police Review*, PC Roy Pollitt of Greater Manchester Police also featured in that magazine's columns. He did a spoof repeat of the research, reproduced here as Table 12.3, largely because it is funny enough to be worth it, but also because you can make some serious points from it. For example, 'being promoted' is included (14) and *is* given a high stress score, reflecting the idea that even potentially pleasant change without control over the outcome of the change is stressful. The affected cynicism of items 4 and 18 are also linked to the intriguingly high stress score of 'Having to do things against your moral principles' in the Bramshill scale.

From G. Gudjonsson and R. Adlam 'A stressful lot', *Police Review*, 14 October 1983. Reprinted with the permission of the publishers, Police Review Publishing Company Limited.

Table 12.2. Mean stress scores

1. Being taken hostage by terrorists	90.1
2. Confronting a person with a gun	82.4
3. Being taken as a hostage in a crime	81.3
4. Negotiating over hostages	69.2
5. Dangerous or violent confrontation	61.2
6. Not being able to rely on your partner	57.3
7. Having to do things against your moral principles	55.9
8. Having to participate in riot control	55.5
9. Job overload	52.1
10. Having to cover up for a colleague	49.6
11. Not getting support from senior officers	48.9
12. Not being accepted by colleagues	48.6
13. Trouble with superiors at work	46.7
14. Long hours	46.6
15. Being involved in brawling incidents	46.0
16. Being caught making a mistake	45.9
17. Shift work	45.9
18. Having a complaint made against you	45.7
19. Giving evidence in court	44.7
20. Having to pass exams	44.5
21. Not being able to express what you feel	44.3
22. Delivering of death messages	43.6
23. Lack of job security	41.3
24. Facing the unpredictable	41.2
25. Seeing mutilated bodies	39.7
26. Being offered bribes	38.2
27. Promotion restrictions	38.5
28. Thwarted ambition	37.3
29. Having to deal with a messy car accident	36.2
30. Inadequate training	35.6
31. Dealing with domestic disturbances	34.8
32. Inadequate pay	34.3
33. Role ambiguity (i.e. lack of clarity about aspects of your job)	34.1
34. Insufficient support by court officials	34.1
35. Promotion course	33.4
36. The possibility of physical injury	33.2
37. Negative community attitudes	32.1
38. Paperwork (e.g. written reports)	31.7
39. Being responsible for people and safety	30.2
40. Rivalry with colleagues of same rank	29.7
41. Having to take command	28.9
42. Boredom	25.5
43. Having to take orders	18.2
44. Giving orders to junior officers	13.4
45. Having to go into people's homes	11.7

Table 12.3. Mean stress scores

1. Being taken hostage   0
(Nobody would want this lot, and even if they did they would soon realize the error of their ways and send them back with a TIC form.)
2. Getting caught up by the plain-clothes inspector while having a pint after time *(Not a teetotaller among them.)*   100
3. Going for a pint after time and finding the landlord has gone to bed   200
4. Being interviewed by the complaints department knowing that you are guilty and not having had time to formulate an alibi   100
5. Telling the wife you are working overtime and having some 'wassock' of a sergeant in the duty office tell her you went home hours ago when she phones to confirm it   80
(1.5 per cent are divorced, separated or just not speaking.)
6. Trying to 'lock up' during a 'tinker' battle when the 6ft 2in 'Paddy' you've just hit shakes his head and smiles   60
(2 per cent are too thick to realize and the other 2 per cent are too thick to be cowards like the rest of us.)
7. Risking ptomaine poisoning in the station canteen   50
(Three are vegetarians, which means they have a salad with their bacon butties, and the others would eat a live carthorse between two slices of bread.)
8. Getting involved in a car chase and having the brakes fail at the last minute   42
(There is not really much danger involved here because usually the dog-van nips in front of you at the last second in an effort to steal the prisoners. It might cause some consternation to the dog if he's looking out of the rear window at the time, but we've used boxers in the force before.)
9. Being cross-examined in court and having the defence ask to look at your pocketbook   3
(Most of them can only print and even then it's so unintelligible that they can't decipher the words themselves.)
10. Having the inspector tell them that A, B and D groups are higher in the league with summonses and arrests   0
(They think they've won when they come bottom.)
11. Helping a voluptuous young woman motorist and, on checking the registration to contact her again, finding the car is registered 'no current keeper'   99
(We've got our doubts about Roger.)

12. Going to the bank two weeks before payday and hoping that the manager won't see you   115
(This one should be self-explanatory.)

13. Having to beat a hasty retreat from a young woman's house when her husband arrives unexpectedly and realizing that you've left your raincoat behind *(No one answered this one because it is still sub judice.)*   100

14. Being promoted   100
(There is a horrendous fear of being put in charge of a relief similar to ours.)

15. Being involved in a riot   0
(This lot cause them, then leave it to others to sort out the mess.)

16. Going on leave and finding on return that everyone has dumped their inquiries in your tray   4
(Most of us just wait for someone else to go on leave.)

17. Being attached to CID   62
(This would entail great expense in buying new clothes because they won't let you in their office dressed in jeans, running shoes and 'I don't have a drink problem' T-shirts.)

18. Having to do things against your moral principles   6
(You've got to have morals first.)

19. Risk of physical injury   0
(It has been known for certain officers to dash into pub fights nose first, clutching criminal injury compensation forms already filled in, and shouting 'Here comes another 400 quid'.)

20. Being transferred to another division   100
(It's taken years for us to condition everyone into thinking we're working.)

From R. Pollitt 'The truth about stress', *Police Review*, 11 November 1983. Reprinted with the permission of the publishers, Police Review Publishing Company Limited.

For purposes of comparison, a more ambitious scale devised in the USA is included as Table 12.4. This scale, reported by James D. Sewell in 1983, should make you thankful that most British officers do not carry guns.

Table 12.4 Law enforcement critical life events scale

Event	Value
1. Violent death of a partner in the line of duty	88
2. Dismissal	85
3. Taking a life in the line of duty	84
4. Shooting someone in the line of duty	81
5. Suicide of an officer who is a close friend	80
6. Violent death of another officer in the line of duty	79
7. Murder committed by a police officer	78
8. Duty-related violent injury (shooting)	76
9. Violent job-related injury to another officer	75
10. Suspension	72
11. Passed over for promotion	71
12. Pursuit of an armed suspect	71
13. Answering a call to a scene involving violent non-accidental death of a child	70
14. Assignment away from family for a long period of time	70
15. Personal involvement in a shooting incident	70
16. Reduction in pay	70
17. Observing an act of police corruption	69
18. Accepting a bribe	69
19. Participating in an act of police corruption	68
20. Hostage situation resulting from aborted criminal action	68
21. Response to a scene involving the accidental death of a child	68
22. Promotion of inexperienced/incompetent officer over you	68
23. Internal affairs investigation against self	66
24. Barricaded suspect	66
25. Hostage situation resulting from a domestic disturbance	65
26. Response to 'officer needs assistance' call	65
27. Duty under a poor supervisor	64
28. Duty-related violent injury (non-shooting)	63
29. Observing an act of police brutality	62
30. Response to 'person with a gun' call	62
31. Unsatisfactory personnel evaluation	62
32. Police-related civil suit	61
33. Riot/crowd control situation	61
34. Failure on a promotional examination	60
35. Suicide of an officer	60

36. Criminal indictment of a fellow officer   60
37. Improperly conducted corruption investigation of another officer   60
38. Shooting incident involving another officer   59
39. Failing grade in police training program   59
40. Response to a felony-in-progress call   58
41. Answering a call to a sexual battery/abuse scene involving a child victim   58
42. Oral promotional review   57
43. Conflict with a supervisor   57
44. Change in departments   56
45. Personal criticism by the press   56
46. Investigation of a political/highly publicized case   56
47. Taking severe disciplinary action against another officer   56
48. Assignment to conduct an internal affairs investigation on another officer   56
49. Interference by political officials in a case   55
50. Written promotional examination   55
51. Departmental misconduct hearing   55
52. Wrecking a departmental vehicle   55
53. Personal use of illicit drugs   54
54. Use of drugs by another officer   54
55. Participating in a police strike   53
56. Undercover assignment   53
57. Physical assault on an officer   52
58. Disciplinary action against partner   52
59. Death notification   51
60. Press criticism of an officer's actions   51
61. Polygraph examination   51
62. Sexual advancement toward you by another officer   51
63. Duty-related accidental injury   51
64. Changing work shifts   50
65. Written reprimand by a supervisor   50
66. Inability to solve a major crime   48
67. Emergency run to 'unknown trouble'   48
68. Personal use of alcohol while on duty   48
69. Inquiry into another officer's misconduct   47
70. Participation in narcotics raid   47
71. Verbal reprimand by a supervisor   47
72. Handling of a mentally/emotionally disturbed person   47
73. Citizen complaint against an officer   47
74. Press criticism of departmental actions/practices   47

114.	Assignment to decoy duty	35
115.	Assignment as partner with officer of opposite sex	35
116.	Assignment to evening shift	35
117.	Assignment of new partner	34
118.	Successful clearance of a case	34
119.	Interrogation session with suspect	33
120.	Departmental budget cut	33
121.	Release of an offender by a jury	33
122.	Overtime duty	29
123.	Letter of recognition from the public	29
124.	Delay in a trial	28
125.	Response to a 'sick or injured person' call	28
126.	Award from a citizens' group	27
127.	Assignment to day shift	26
128.	Work on holiday	26
129.	Making a routine arrest	26
130.	Assignment to a two-man car	25
131.	Call involving juveniles	25
132.	Routine patrol stop	25
133.	Assignment to a single-man car	25
134.	Call involving the arrest of a female	24
135.	Court appearance (misdemeanor)	24
136.	Working a traffic accident	23
137.	Dealing with a drunk	23
138.	Pay raise	23
139.	Overtime pay	22
140.	Making a routine traffic stop	22
141.	Vacation	20
142.	Issuing a traffic citation	20
143.	Court appearance (traffic)	19
144.	Completion of a routine report	13

From James D. Sewell 'The development of a critical life events scale for law enforcement', *Journal of Police Science and Administration*, *11(1)*, 113–114. Reprinted with the permission of the International Association of Chiefs of Police, P.O. Box 6010, 13 Firstfield Road, Gaithersburg, Maryland 20878 USA.

The essential reason for our being interested in the morality issue is that it bears on what we regard as probably the fundamental dilemma of police work: the tension between the ideals of due process and crime control. On the one hand doing everything necessary to reduce crime, and on the other acting strictly within the letter of the law, not taking any short cuts, not breaching suspects' rights in any way. This means that the police officer is treading a moral

tightrope, and even the best acrobat falls off sometimes. We feel this
tension is one of the reasons for the oft-noted cynicism of many
young officers. The high stress potential of having to do things
against your moral principles could well be linked to this sort of
problem.

Some other American research on police stress identifies child
abuse, domestic violence and 'unresponsive judges' as the three
most generally stressing situations. 'Uncooperative prosecutors'
also had high stress potential, and this again might be taken to illustrate the tensions between the requirements of procedural exactness
and effectiveness in crime clearance.

Different stressors for different people

We have laboured the point that although you can say that certain
sorts of situation are generally more stressful than others, whether
or not any particular individual finds a situation stressful depends
on their perception of it. Fools enter where angels fear to tread
because fools cannot see the frightening aspects of the situation. The
values which led you to choose a career in the police service no
doubt reflect your personality. Values and personality affect what
you regard as stressful. In some American work, officers were
divided into groups on the basis of what they said were the values
which led to their career choice.

- The first type of officer chose the job primarily for *personal
  reward*, emphasizing salary, fringe benefits, job security and
  working conditions.

- The second sort of officer was *people oriented*, emphasizing as
  reasons for career choice protecting the public, providing a service and working with people rather than things.

- The third type was oriented towards a *professional career*, stressing as reasons high prestige, independence on the job, the use of
  professional skills and advancement to a position of authority.

The central point is that the different types of officer differed in
what they regarded as stressful. For example, although officers of all
types found weapon calls and domestic violence stressful, *professional career* oriented officers found situations endangering their
personal safety particularly stressful. People oriented officers found
conflicting job demands especially stressful. Table 12.5 summarizes
the differences between types of officer in what are regarded as high
stress and low stress situations. We would like readers to classify

themselves as one of the three types, and to see whether their general pattern of stresses corresponds to those found in Table 12.5. If it does, this is doubly useful. First, it demonstrates the differences in reactions to stress situations we have been so keen to emphasize. Second, and following from that, it should alert you to the fact that your colleagues with different values find different situations a source of stress. What is more, different sorts of officer react to stress in different ways. Personal reward oriented officers are distinctive in developing ulcers and alcoholism, people oriented officers react with arguments in the home and divorce and professional career oriented officers with moodiness and nervous anxiety. Of course there are substantial *individual* differences superimposed on 'type' differences. People are more than just types. But the point is well made that police officers differ in what they regard as stressful and how they react to stress.

The differences just described may be of significance in the 'hazing' of young police officers, where difficult situations are 'set up' by their new colleagues to see if the young officer will react in a way which allows him or her to be trusted thereafter. Usually this set-up is one of physical confrontation. However, it should be recalled that different *types* of situation will be the acid test for different types of officer. Officers who acquit themselves less than well in the test situation may sail through other types of situation which stress their colleagues. This brings into focus a topic which we think important. This is the subject of the stresses experienced by women police officers, both in the course of their job and in the experiences of a woman in a male-dominated profession. The particular sources of stress, both from the job and from fellow officers, have not yet been studied, to our knowledge. You may have your own ideas about this. If you are a man, ask the next woman officer you spend time with what she thinks.

How to recognize stress

Much of the Police Federation's recent concern with stress in the workplace seems centred on stress-inducing and stress-maintaining management styles. Although the stressed response depends upon individual perceptions of the situation, are there any signs of 'stress centres' in the organization which suggest that something about the organization is causing the stress? Nico van Dijkhuizen of the Royal Netherlands Navy (we mention this to show that the psychologist concerned comes from a disciplined service) in 1981 provided a useful checklist of signs of stress:

Table 12.5. Sources of stress by officer type

ORGANIZATIONAL SOURCES OF STRESS BY POLICE TYPE

	Personal/reward oriented	People oriented	Professionally oriented
Unresponsive judges	H	H	H
Uncooperative prosecutors	H	H	H
Lack of recognition and rewards	H	L	L
Insensitive supervisors	L	L	H
Conflicting job demands	L	H	L

PERSONAL SAFETY SOURCES OF STRESS BY POLICE TYPE

	Personal/reward oriented	People oriented	Professionally oriented
Domestic violence	H	H	H
Weapons call	H	H	H
Fights in public places	L	L	H
Breaking and entering in progress	L	L	H
Hot pursuit	H	L	H
Traffic stops	L	L	L
Silent alarm calls	L	L	L

OTHER-RELATED SOURCES OF STRESS BY POLICE TYPE

	Personal/reward oriented	People oriented	Professionally oriented
Child abuse	H	H	H
Homicide	L	H	L
Rape	L	L	H
Personal injury or accidents	L	L	H
Drownings	H	L	H
In-home injury	L	L	L
Assault investigation	L	L	L
Burglary investigation	L	L	L

Note: H = high; L = low.

From P.A. Russo, A.S. Engel and S.H. Hatting (1983) Police and occupational stress: An empirical investigation. In R.R. Bennett (ed.) *Police at Work: Policy Issues and Analysis*. Reprinted with the permission of the publishers, Sage Inc., Beverly Hills.

- decreased work performance
- high absenteeism
- high staff turnover
- irritability and much interpersonal conflict
- less social support from colleagues
- family problems (see, for instance, the sad anonymous note about this in the *Police Review*, 10 February 1984)
- increased smoking or drinking
- sleeplessness
- changed clothing habits (becoming more scruffy or less scruffy)
- changed eating habits (forgetting meals, eating fast or excessively)
- high cholesterol levels
- fight–flight reactions (attacking and ridiculing or withdrawing from contact with others).

Clearly these features will exhibit themselves in different people in different kinds of environment. Some will thrive in situations which make others chain-smoking, irritable, illness-prone wrecks. However, if some of these features are pretty general, a *stress centre* can be identified, with stress reduction being required to take an organizational rather than an individual form. The choice between organizational and individual approaches to the problem of stress is one that we shall address in the next and last section of this chapter.

What to do about it?

We admit to a general preference for organizational as opposed to individual approaches to stress problems, although the two should obviously be regarded as complementing each other. However, when the same fuse keeps blowing in your house or car, there is something wrong with the circuit of which it is a part. Blaming a dud batch of fuses is not a sensible thing to do. Aircraft accident investigation teams analyse accidents on an 'all-systems-involved' basis, with the aim of taking all possible steps to improve design *before* blaming the operator. We think this is an approach which has a lot to commend it. To take an example from another topic relevant to police work, we think it is crucial in the analysis of intruder alarms and other security hardware, where blaming the hardware user gets in the way of designing foolproof equipment.

The reason for stressing organizational rather than individual change is that once you have blamed a *person*, you no longer seek to improve the design of the *environment*. In the same way, regarding people as stress-prone means that you no longer seek to modify the environment so that it does not subject people to so much stress. However, we cannot reasonably neglect ways of changing the individual, although we cannot cover the topic properly and therefore refer the reader to our suggestions for further reading at the end of the chapter.

A mention was made earlier of the feeling of helplesness. This is the perception of a lack of control over the events of life. We think that the perception of some control is a basic human *need*, but people vary hugely in the amount of control they see themselves as having. You must be aware from your personal experience that some people dive into new jobs convinced that any problems will yield to their iron will. Others take on jobs equally convinced that they will not. It is clear that this sense of control, which can be enhanced by appropriate training or experience, does reduce stress. Retirement planning, for example, seems to alleviate the stresses of that particular life change by giving people a sense of control over what is happening. People who become quickly aware of their own internal body states are less prone to stress-induced illness, because once they know what is happening inside their body they can do something about it.

Of course feelings of control are a two-edged sword. What happens when it becomes obvious that really you are not in control? What happens when you start to mend your car in a spirit of confidence and control, and end up with the bits all over the garage floor? It is not too hard to guess that the research shows that you feel particularly depressed over the discovery that you are not really in control after all. Then the only answer lies in training or supervised experience. We think there are some lessons there for police trainers and tutor constables.

Other individual approaches to stress concentrate on relaxation. While the ability to relax is an obvious and desirable way of reducing the impact of stress, it is not enough. It is essentially shutting the stable door after the horse has bolted. Hence our emphasis is on organizational change.

Nico Van Dijkhuizen emphasizes organizational change in response to stress. He describes three phases in an organization's strategy to cope with stress. They are *research*, *classification* and *attack*. Research involves looking through organizations to identify stress centres (i.e. centres which are stressful for a number of the people who work in them). He then suggests that the next stage is classification, distinguishing four broad levels at which problems might be addressed. Restated in ways which are directly relevant to police work, these are:

- Changing the structure, lines of accountability or communication patterns within an organization. For example, an ambiguous system of communication places each officer in a position of helplessness.
- Spelling out how a good job performance is recognized as such.
- Working on the level of the worker's *role*; what are the pressures being exerted on an individual occupying a role position?
- On the level of the individual: are the right people being selected, are they being trained as well as they could, and are the features which lead to their promotion ones which allow them to perform consistently at the higher level?

Once the stress is classified as avoidable or unavoidable, changes can be effected by changing, for example:

- equipment and office/station design
- changing lines of communication within or between departments (of course police traditions and culture allow only a limited amount of this)
- changing individual patterns of responsibility within the organization
- clarification of tasks and responsibilities
- increasing support from superiors and colleagues
- reorganizing selection, training and promotion procedures to incorporate the lessons to be learned from stressed people.

Although the above analyses are necessarily along fairly general lines, they will serve their purpose, which is to show that we are not helpless in the face of stress. There are things which may be done to make things better. And as we showed above, the sense of helplessness is itself a source of stress!

Review notes

Police officers are prone to stress, and concern is growing about this. Situations vary in their capacity to *evoke* stress, and people vary in the kind of situation they experience as stressful. Police stressors include management behaviour to a surprisingly high extent.

Officers differ in what they find stressful, according to whether they joined the force for personal reward, or because they were people oriented or wanted a professional career. These types of officer react differently to different situations.

Factors indicating stress are described. Many organizations have stress centres, where the organization could take steps to reduce pressure on people. It is important to redesign organizations in preference to changing people, although there are ways of reducing the impact of unavoidable stress on the individual.

References

Anon. (1984) Married to the Job. *Police Review*, 10 February, 270–271.
Holmes, T.H. and Rahe, R.H. (1967) The social readjustment rating scale. *Journal of Psychosomatic Research*, 11, 213–218.
Gudjonsson, G. and Adlam, R. (1983) A stressful lot. *Police Review*, 14 October, 1981.
McAuley, L. (1981) The policeman's private agony. *The Sunday Times*, 18 January.
Pollitt, R. (1983) The truth about stress. *Police Review* , 11 November, 2115.
Sewell, J.D. (1983) The development of a critical life events scale for law enforcement. *Journal of Police Science and Administration*, 11(1), 113–114.
van Dijkhuizen, N. (1981) Towards organisational coping with stress. In J. Marshall and C.L. Cooper (eds) *Coping with Stress at Work*. Farnborough: Gower.

Further reading

Marshall, J. and Cooper, C.L. (eds) (1981) *Coping with Stress at Work*. Farnborough: Gower.
Tyrer, P. (1980) *How to Cope with Stress*. London: Sheldon.

Chapter 13

Crime Fears, Crime Victims and Community Contacts

Cancer is a bad thing in two ways. First, it makes people very ill, and kills a large number of those contracting it. Second, it makes people very afraid. Whether the amount of human suffering resulting from the fear is less than the suffering resulting from the disease itself is a moot point. You have probably seen both the fact and the fear of cancer. If you have, you will surely agree with us that both cause great misery.

What, you might think, has this got to do with crime? We think that when talking about the twin miseries of fear and fact, precisely the same is true of crime as of cancer. The fear of crime, like the fear of cancer, is itself a major problem, and it is one of which the police should be aware. It is difficult to ask a police officer to play down the fear of crime. This is because the more crime is feared, the more serious the crime problem is seen to be, and the more important is the police officer's role in society.

But consider the consequences of crime fear. Certain areas, notably in cities, become virtual no-go areas after dark. Taxis carry those who can afford it across areas regarded as dangerous, leaving the public transport system freer for offenders to go about their business undisturbed. Fearful and suspicious people become more distrustful and withdrawn, and then 'keep themselves to themselves', creating a population more distrustful and withdrawn, less willing to get involved in the affairs of others, and more lonely.

People's fears are not only for themselves. How many hours do children spend indoors, how much happiness do they lose, and how much do they risk injury from frustrated parents in claustrophobic flats? These extra risks stem in part from parents' fears about what might happen to them if they play outside, since 'There's such a lot of funny people about nowadays'. How often do middle-class families leave city homes from fear for their children or themselves? How much does the education and social life of those who remain suffer in an area seen to be 'going downhill'? Truly, fear of crime is an important social problem.

There are three aspects of crime fear which police officers should know about:

- The people who are the most afraid are the people who are the least likely to be victimized.
- Among the factors which make people afraid, 'incivilities' (discourtesies and signs of disorder) are important.
- We are living in times when the 'protect yourself' industries are flourishing, and their appeal is based largely on stimulating crime fear. This has implications for police work.

The first of the three findings, that fear and risk do not go hand in hand, is perhaps the most surprising. The people who are most afraid of crime (older females) are the least likely to fall victim to it. The group least afraid of crime (young males) are the ones who are most likely to become crime victims. All the studies which have looked at this issue have arrived at the same conclusion. Women are more fearful of crime than men. In a British study in 1982, it was found that 41 per cent of women living in inner cities feel very unsafe walking alone at night in their neighbourhood. Older women in particular feel afraid. Although burglary is a major cause of fear, fear of predatory street crime is perhaps the most insidious for social life. Rape, attempted rape, sexual assault, robbery, attempted robbery, theft and attempted theft where the victim and offender are in physical contact are the component offences of this crime type. All relevant research shows that older women have a low risk of victimization in predatory street crime.

Those of you reading this carefully and drawing on your own experience will immediately see a problem in this research. Perhaps, you will say, it is *because* the old ladies are afraid that they do not fall victim. If they avoid dark passages, get home before dark and lock their front doors behind them, they *are* going to be less likely to become victims. But that is only because they take all these steps to prevent victimization. The only way of sorting this problem out is to see whether the older women who *do* go out in inner cities (and do it often and go by public transport), are in fact more victimized. Fortunately, there is good research evidence here. The risk of victimization of older women is not high. It is much lower than the risk run by younger people with much less active social lives. For example, the risk of victimization of older women who went out three or more times a week by 'risky' means is 35 per 100,000. This contrasts with a risk of 107 per 100,000 for young men who go out only once or twice a week by 'risky' means.

Older women are not as likely to be victimized as their level of fear would suggest. The fear of predatory crime among older women *is* in general unreasonably high. That there are pockets of truly high risk is acknowledged, but they are pockets, even within decayed inner city areas. Of course the police cannot remove people's fears by just telling them that there is no reason for it. Nor can the police do very much in the face of media presentations which often seem designed to heighten fear. The pictures in daily newspapers of beaten old ladies are shocking, and worth a thousand frightening words. We would not suggest that terrible crimes against old people should receive no publicity. They are newsworthy. However, they are also very rare and much more could be done to emphasize their rarity. (It is a paradox that if old women were beaten up every day, it would not make news.)

Some parts of the media are now trying to treat crime issues responsibly. The BBC TV *Crimewatch UK* programme emphasizes how rare are the terrible crimes with which they deal. The National Association of Victim Support Schemes (NAVSS) also takes a highly responsible line, taking responsibility for helping victims without increasing fear of crime. No matter the limits to what the police officer can do, he or she can always reassure. Officers should resist glamourizing their jobs to receptive audiences of older people by overstating the prevalence and viciousness of crimes.

There has been speculation by psychologists that older people are fearful particularly because there is no one to whom they can turn for help if they do become victims. They also feel deeply a lack of anyone who can reassure them. If police officers can present themselves as people to respect, people to reassure the older person and to involve neighbours and acquaintances in this process, this must be helpful in removing at least one reason for crime fear. The reader is invited to bear this in mind when thinking about crisis intervention (see Chapter 9).

A little earlier, we distinguished between fear for one's own safety and worry about the safety of other people. This sort of worry is greatest, not among old people, but among middle-aged men and, only slightly less, middle-aged women. Of course these are the years in a family life cycle when young and teenage children are likely to be in the home.

In dealings with the worried and fearful, experienced officers come to learn that the fear and worry can show itself as snappiness, shortness of temper, unpredictability or withdrawal. The less experienced officer who wishes to be most sensitive in his or her dealings should bear this in mind, and know that the occasional deep breath and refusal to rise to the bait will be needed.

Another factor in crime fear is experience. People who have themselves been victims and people who know other people who have been victimized show more concern about crime. However, the link between victimization and fear is not a simple one. A good example of this is the obscene telephone call. Receiving such a call heightens fears of some, but not all, crimes. If you place yourself in the shoes of the recipient of an obscene call, the things you would fear include burglary of your empty house (he knows when I am out, and if he got my number from the phone book he could burgle the house, perhaps for items of personal clothing), sexual assault (obviously, given the nature of the call) and assault or mugging (he could get angry with me putting the phone down, or he could know the way I come home on payday).

In fact these are precisely the offences which women who have had obscene calls fear more than do other women. In reality, getting an obscene phone call does not increase a woman's chance of falling victim to other offences. The offence seems to be a self-contained one. This is a very important reassurance to give to women receiving these calls. What is more, it is important, particularly for policemen, to sympathize with the fears the calls cause, and to spend time talking about them. If may be tempting to dismiss these fears. After all, the victim could put the phone down at any time, and could leave it off the hook. The offence has a very modest maximum penalty and you may wonder what all the fuss is about. Just remember the fears before fobbing the victim off with 'There, there, but there's nothing much we can do about it'.

Another sort of event, besides crime victimization, seems to be of crucial importance in generating fear of crime. This is incivility. Let us return to our analogy with cancer to explain the significance of the idea. Most people, most of the time, do not have cancer, yet people are afraid because of the little signs that just might be early symptoms of cancer. Women with what feel like lumps in the breast, smokers with hacking coughs, people with chronic indigestion, constipation or weight loss are all examples. The odds are very much that these symptoms will not be confirmed as cancer, but they are what cause the fear that one might have cancer. Like cancer, crime is a rare event for the individual citizen – although a lot less rare than we would like it to be. In the same way that we look for signs which we can interpret as cancer and then worry about the full-blown cancer that might develop from them, so we look for or become aware of signs of disorder or incivility from which we fear real crime will develop. What are these signs of incivility? Three which were selected by Wesley Skogan and Michael Maxfield (1981) are:

- groups of teenagers hanging out on the streets
- buildings or storefronts abandoned or burned out
- vandalism (for example, children breaking windows or writing on walls).

Although British examples might be a little more subtle than these North American ones, the sense of 'incivility' is easy enough to grasp. A good example of the 'feel' of people's views about these in-civilities comes from three older men interviewed by Skogan and Maxfield. They were asked whether they were afraid of young peo-ple. They answered, 'Not afraid, exactly, but leery, extremely leery of young people, that you never know what's on a young person's mind. Then one of them said that a lot of young people he knows, some of the things they do are just to be mean, just to be ornery, it serves no purpose, it's really senseless.'

Ask the older members of your own family, and they may well come out with something similar. It is not that groups of teenagers necessarily do anything, it is what they *might* do. The gang of teenagers on the corner is to crime what weight loss is to cancer – a symptom which seldom leads to anything, but which does frighten you. No doubt you can think of other incivilities, like stray dogs in packs and uncleared glass on paths, beggars and people drinking in the street.

It is very difficult to think of a role for individual police officers which is directed to reducing incivilities generally. In 1984, Michael Maxfield concluded his analysis of crime fear in England and Wales thus:

Policies to reduce crime fear in inner cities are attractive, and potentially beneficial. At present, it seems most appropriate to integrate such actions with existing policies – including victim support schemes, council housing renewal, police response to service calls from the public, Neighbourhood Watch and other crime prevention schemes. The benefits of an approach which integrates fear reduction and crime prevention are twofold: it maximizes the utilization of scarce resources; and it avoids many of the political difficulties that may accompany actions that appear to address fear instead of crime.

This is a balanced conclusion. Obviously the police have an important role to play in its support.

The third point about crime fear is the way in which it is currently being used by private security firms to drum up business. Indeed, much police recruitment and crime prevention literature is just as bad. Clearly the only way in which fear of crime can be permanently defeated is by creating communities (such as already exist in most rural and some urban areas) which are seen to be safe and where people on the streets are not a cause for fear. Yet what we have seen is a flight of the well-to-do to the suburbs, or to heavily guarded prestige estates within the city. (In 1985 Prime Minister Margaret Thatcher bought a house on such an estate.) At the same time, your local high street will probably be boasting a new shop selling security hardware, with a display in the window emphasizing how common burglary is. In today's local newspaper there are as many classified advertisements under 'Home Securities' as 'Holiday Accommodation' and more than under 'Driving Tuition' 'Lost and Found' and 'Deaths'. We are told 'enjoy security with 24-hour protection', even though it is clear that security furniture is very far from being a complete protection against burglary. The police are named in these advertisements. Devices are described as 'police/insurance approved' and some senior officers on retirement go into careers in alarm companies. So what?

Our central point is that while the police service is engaged in what it likes to call the fight against crime, there are people in the community making fear of crime worse, and using the police's name in doing so. The police ought also to be engaged in a fight against the fear of crime. The service can be helpful in providing reassurance to those who are overly fearful, and also use their influence with other bodies (like the Press Council and the Advertising Standards Authority) to keep the crime problem in proportion. Crime really *is* still a rare event for most people in almost all areas. Taking crimes of burglary as an example (some of which are in any event insurance frauds) a burglary happens in the *average* English household once every forty years. Put another way, on 14 609 days out of 14 610, your house will *not* get burgled. It still makes sense not to invite burglary, but the risk itself must surely be kept in proportion.

This is, of course, not to deny the existence of some crime-prone areas where the burglary risk is enormously greater than 1 in 40 – as well as some crime-free areas where it is enormously less than 1 in 40.

We conclude this section with a quotation from Michael Gottfredson (1984) about crime risks and fears. He writes that one thing which stands out:

> is the relative rarity of serious criminal victimisation. It seems likely that at least some of the concern about crime and victimisation among the public is caused by uncertainty – uncertainty about one's chances of falling victim, uncertainty about when and where it is likely to happen, and uncertainty about how it would be dealt with if it did happen. The data can help the public know that crime is relatively rare, that most of the crime which does occur is not particularly serious in the sense of bodily harm or financial loss ... and that a small segment of the population seems particularly prone. Perhaps the single best example of this relates to criminal victimisation of the elderly ... The elderly do not face the greatest risk from personal household crime – in fact the reverse is true – it is the young who are most at risk.

The essence of our message is that the police should do what they can, individually and collectively, to reduce crime fear. A simple example concerns the use of sirens. Every time a police vehicle siren is heard, fearful people will assume a serious crime has been committed. If the use of the siren could be restricted to occasions where it is really necessary, this would have a fear-reducing effect. Every time a police officer emphasizes the realistic good points of an area, or seems relaxed on duty, talking to groups of youths in a friendly way, the threat perceived is imperceptibly reduced. It is easy to over-state the effects, but every little helps. Larger, organizational changes are necessary for more substantial improvements to be made. In George Orwell's novel *Animal Farm* one of the most attractive characters was a carthorse who thought the answer to all problems was to work harder, when the real problem lay in the way the farm was organized. He died of overwork. The actions of individual officers help. The re-orientation of the organization is necessary for major change.

Dealing with victims

Much of the material in Chapter 9 provides some information about techniques of dealing with the victims of crime. We think it worth-while to devote a short section to the topic of why you should deal effectively with victims of crime, and we now develop the theme in the context of a discussion of dealing with members of the public more generally.

When victims call the police, they are in a state of confusion and not very clear what they want the police to do, except make them feel better. There is also evidence that the police believe victims want an arrest or their property back and there is immediate mis-communication as a result. The police also expect victims to have a clear idea of what has occurred, what has been lost, and what should be done, and this is not always realistic. Information and advice given by the police at the initial visit are rarely taken in at that point, and a return visit from the police or a volunteer from a victim support scheme the following day can be much more effective.

While many crime victims are very matter-of-fact about the whole thing, many others are very upset indeed, and respond to the trauma for a long time afterwards. Burglary victims are particularly dis-tressed. Fears that the offender may return are common, but this will rarely be communicated to the police. Helen Reeves, National Officer of NAVSS, argues that the police will rarely be told about these fears, and it may be helpful for them to anticipate by suggest-ing that 'many people do worry about the offender returning, but there is little danger'. This gives the victim 'permission' to express the fears experienced, stopping the danger that they will feel abnor-mal if they are very upset. Some burglary victims find that they can-not stop shaking when they come home to a house they once found broken into. Others have difficulty sleeping there. Some react with tears and anger immediately. Some behave irrationally but under-standably. Taking a bath after being raped destroys evidence but can also make the victim feel slightly less bad after an unspeakably bad experience.

Many victims feel a loss of a sense of control over a world they thought they had pretty well weighed up. This sense of helpless-ness, which we referred to earlier as an important component of stress, is also an important cause of depression in crime victims. What it also means is that steps the police officer can take to make the victim feel more in control of the situation are always a good thing, although no guarantees should be given. A second victimiza-tion after you thought you were safe can be shattering. However, crime prevention advice after a burglary allows the victim to *do* something, to regain *some* control. Another part of treating victims well is keeping them informed. Research suggests that two of the main complaints crime victims have are:

- That the investigating officers seem indifferent to what has happened.
- That no one tells them if or how the investigation is proceeding.

In short, victims do not expect miracles. They do not necessarily expect the police to catch an offender – but they do require the police to show some interest in what has happened.

Officers should remember that although they may have experienced the aftermath of crimes often, the victim has not. Falling victim to crime can change the habits of a lifetime, and will certainly affect future opinions, including opinions of the police. Just showing it matters to you (see Chapter 2 for details of how) is important. You should also be alive to the fact that any information, even if it amounts to nothing, helps. If the police force wishes to maintain good relations with crime victims, it will call them back, even if there is nothing new to say. Although most members of the public *do* think the police do a good job, it is troubling that research suggests that fewer victims of crime think that. This may mean that, as a general rule, the police are not now handling victims of crime as well as they might.

If we asked you which groups of people get most upset by crime victimization, the odds are that you would say old people. Perhaps you would say women in general and perhaps you might talk of social class, with the upper classes, who have experienced less of the hurly-burly of street life, being more upset. The fact is that predicting which victims will be upset by crime is not easy. The great practical point here is that a police officer should not assume that a young lower-class male is all right, and will take things in his stride. Likewise an upper-crust old lady *could* be out chasing the fox the same afternoon, with only a few choice phrases as a reminder of what she thinks of the offender. The *Police Review* editorial of 3 February 1984 makes the point admirably.

> Present plans to complete many investigations of crime on the first and only visit may well improve police efficiency, but they need to be accompanied by a true realisation of the needs of the victims. Some may need comfort, some may want to talk about it, some may just want information. But the teenager living alone who has his meter broken open, the one-man business

whose equipment is stolen overnight ... have one thing in common: their experience is too important *to them* to be translated into nothing more than a police statistic.

There are now many victim support schemes up and down the country which provide crime victims with a sympathetic ear and practical help. One of the big obstacles is the police. They have to make the referral of victims to the schemes. If they operate on the basis that only old ladies get upset by crime, and refer just old ladies, lots of people who get to the scheme will not need it, and many of those not referred to the scheme will need it but will not get it. There are only two sensible referral procedures. One is to refer all victims of non-trivial crime. The other is to refer only those people who are upset. Because it is not always easy to tell who is upset, or when there will be a delayed reaction or trouble with repair or an insurance claim, we prefer the first approach. We think it is more important that those who need support get it than that those who do not are offered it. If you do not know of a local victim support scheme, write to NAVSS, 17a Electric Lane, Brixton, London SW9 8JT.

A word on experience

Police officers with a lot of experience do differ from those with little experience. It is a lot more difficult to put your finger on the precise nature of the difference. Do experienced officers know more 'wrinkles'; do they differ in the decisions they make in difficult situations; or is it a combination of these and other things? Whatever it is, Lord Scarman and others obviously think it is important in the policing of difficult areas, and regret the high proportion of inexperienced officers on the streets in those areas. In an article in *The Sunday Times* of 19 April 1981, a senior Metropolitan officer is quoted: 'There is a feeling that some young officers have not helped the situation, and it may be time to think about replacing them with older coppers.'

This is not to say that everything that experience teaches you is a good thing. Doctors in earlier times 'bled' patients to remove some unspecified pressure or poison from the patient's system. No doubt more experienced doctors bled people more efficiently. However, for many diseases bleeding patients is worse than useless. Those experienced doctors were not therefore more likely to save lives. However, we do happen to believe that experienced police officers have a street wisdom that is of enormous value. What we really regret is that so much of basic training teaches people to behave unlike experienced police officers. In disputes, experienced officers resolve things by making an arrest less often than do inexperienced officers. Yet our experience and impression is that in training school simulated problems are set up to be resolved by arrest (and, incidentally, young officers often humiliated in the process, but that is a different can of worms).

Training in ways that experience will contradict is a waste of time, and we think a lot of time is wasted in this way in police training. However, the real reason for including this short section here is to say that one way in which experienced officers differ is that they spend longer on each incident they deal with. They thus give victims more time to come to terms with what has happened, and give the impression that someone does care what has happened. It seems to us that this lesson which experience usually teaches (not all experienced officers have learned from their experience!) is a valuable one. With victims, take your time. It will reduce the likelihood of the victim's dissatisfaction, and may even lead to a letter of appreciation.

Contacts with members of the public

In a recent major national survey, it was found that 49 per cent of a representative sample of the public had contact with a police officer during the survey period (just over a year). The majority of these contacts were initiated by the member of the public, and most contacts did not involve crime. Thus, as you knew already, service calls are the subject of more police–public contacts than crime. It is of particular interest that even in urban Northern Ireland, an area where you would think 'service' contacts were least likely to predominate, they still do. What you may not have realized is the size of the percentage of the public which had contact with the police in a year or so – virtually 50 per cent. These facts, taken together, suggest that the scope for influencing public attitude to the police by routine behaviour is enormous.

Why bother? Primarily because the extent to which the police rely on public information and assistance in clearing crime is huge. For instance, attitudes to the police are influential in the decision to report less serious crime in the first place. Good relations between police and public also make for an easier life – calls for police accountability are loudest in areas where public trust and confidence in the police are lowest.

What is it about police behaviour that annoys the public, and in what sort of contact does this show itself most? Taking the second part of the question first, look at Table 13.1, which summarizes the relationship between type of contact and annoyance with the police. It is clear that people stopped by the police either on foot or in vehicles are most often annoyed. A finding we regard as particularly important is that *a quarter* of those of those who approached the police themselves were annoyed! In other words, one in four members of the public choosing to approach a police officer were annoyed by the exchange. These are people on whom the police will rely for information at other times. What is it about police behaviour which pleased or displeased members of the public? When members of the public pronounced themselves pleased, officers were commended for their efficiency, helpfulness and understanding (the latter two being aspects we have highlighted in our discussion on contacts with crime victims).

Table 13.1. Annoyance with the police in past five years, by type of contact

	% annoyed with police
Contact with police during recall period:	
Stopped on foot	46
Stopped in vehicle	38
Approached by police only as a suspect	35
Approached by police only as a non-suspect	24
Approached police themselves	24
Not stopped on foot by police	16
Not stopped in a vehicle by police	14
All respondents	17

Weighted data; unweighted N = 6329

From K. Heal, R. Tarling and J. Burrows (1985) *Policing Today*. London: HMSO. Reprinted with the permission of the Controller of Her Majesy's Stationery Office.

Table 13.2 sets out the causes of annoyance with the police. The striking point is that fully a third of the reasons for annoyance concerned the police officer's *attitude*. In one third of the police–public contacts, then, public goodwill was thrown away purely because of officers' attitudes. If you think the public is hypersensitive, we will disagree with you! Both authors of this book have had, in one capacity or another, extensive contact with the police, almost all collaborative. Yet both of us have vivid recollections of street encounters with officers who would have alienated a saint by their attitude, and memory of these contacts still produces bad feeling. You must recognize such officers among your colleagues. We only hope that some of them will read this, and perhaps recognize themselves.

Table 13.2 Causes of annoyance with the police in the past five years (per cent)

Alleged misconduct:	
Undue use of force	9
Corruption/malpractice	6
Wrongful arrest or stop	14
False accusation	12
Inefficiency:	
Inaction	15
Wrong action	12
Attitude	33
Other annoyance	8

Weighted data; unweighted N = 1327

From K. Heal, R. Tarling and J. Burrows (1985) *Policing Today*. London: HMSO. Reprinted with the permission of the Controller of Her Majesy's Stationery Office.

What is worth knowing from a book on the psychology of police work is that even alienated people report very serious crimes. Both the Policy Studies Institute research on the Metropolitan Police and some unpublished work on the Royal Ulster Constabulary confirm that. These are the two forces in the United Kingdom which one might regard as being most alienated from the people they serve. Yet even here, people say they would report serious crimes to the police. In other words, having an alienated public will not save you the trouble of having serious crimes to solve. All it will keep from you is the information about crime generally and the resources from public goodwill which you need to solve them.

Review notes

The fear of crime and the fact of crime are twin social problems. The elderly are more afraid of crime than their rates of victimization suggest they should be.

Signs of social disorder, like youths hanging around and broken windows also evoke crime fear. The security industry seems intent on building up crime fear. The police are in a good position to recognize and soothe crime fear.

Some crimes which may seem trivial from the outside may have severe emotional impact. The police should recognize the distress of victims. Victims above all seem to want an acknowledgement of the seriousness of what has happened, and information about the progress of investigations. They do not expect miracles. Experienced officers spend longer in dealing with people than do less experienced officers.

Many citizens become annoyed with police officers during contacts. In around one third of these cases, it is the officer's *attitude* that causes the annoyance. Goodwill is thus thown away.

References

Clarke, R.V.G., Ekblom, P. Hough, M. and Mayhew, P. (1985) Elderly victims of crime and exposure to risk. *Howard Journal of Criminal Justice*, 24, 1–9.
Gottfredson, M.R. (1984) *Victims of Crime: The Dimensions of Risk*. (Home Office Research Study 81.) London: HMSO.
Maxfield, M.G. (1984) *Fear of Crime in England and Wales*. (Home Office Research Study 78.) London: HMSO.
Skogan, W.G. and Maxfield, M.G. (1981) *Coping with Crime*. Beverly Hills: Sage.

Further reading

Skogan, W.G. and Maxfield, M.G. (1981) *Coping with Crime*. Beverly Hills: Sage.

Index